Brahms's

Vocal Duets and
Quartets with Piano

Brahms's
Vocal Duets and Quartets with Piano

A GUIDE WITH FULL TEXTS
AND TRANSLATIONS

Lucien Stark

Indiana
University
Press

BLOOMINGTON AND INDIANAPOLIS

Frontispiece: Title-page drawing by Ludwig Richter (1803–1884) for *Hausmusik,*
fifty settings by Wilhelm Heinrich Riehl (1823–1897) of texts
by German poets (Stuttgart and Augsburg: J. G. Cotta, 1855)

The paper used in this publication meets the minimum
requirements of American National Standard for Information
Sciences—Permanence of Paper for Printed Library Materials, ANSI Z39.48-1984.

MANUFACTURED IN THE UNITED STATES OF AMERICA

Library of Congress Cataloging-in-Publication Data
Stark, Lucien, date
   Brahms's vocal duets and quartets with piano : a guide with full
texts and translations /
Lucien Stark.
       p.   cm.
   Includes bibliographical references and index.
   ISBN 0-253-33402-0 (cloth : alk. paper)
    1. Brahms, Johannes, 1833–1897—Vocal music.   2. Vocal ensembles
with piano—Analysis, appreciation.   I. Title.
MT115.B73S7   1998
782.42168'092—dc21   97-45142
  1   2   3   4   5   03   02   01   00   99   98   MN

To Paul, Vida, Justin, and Elena

CONTENTS

PREFACE

It hardly seems possible that within the oeuvre of so popular and so thoroughly studied a composer as Brahms most of an entire genre of works should sink into neglect, unperformed. Yet, of the duets and quartets for solo voices with piano, only the *Liebeslieder* and, to a lesser extent, the *Neue Liebeslieder* and *Zigeunerlieder* could currently be described as familiar. It is my sincere hope that this guide might help to remedy that situation.

Not surprisingly, there is only a small literature that treats specifically of the duets or quartets. Many of the works listed in the bibliography are therefore only tangentially relevant, but all have been helpful to some extent. Citations within the text are abbreviated.

Three resources have been indispensable:

(1) Brahms's correspondence, particularly the two volumes in English of *Letters of Clara Schumann and Johannes Brahms, 1853–1896*, edited by Berthold Litzmann and anonymously translated (New York: Vienna House, 1973; reprint of the 1927 London publication); *Johannes Brahms: The Herzogenberg Correspondence*, edited by Max Kalbeck, translated by Hannah Bryant (New York: Vienna House, 1971); and *Johannes Brahms and Theodor Billroth: Letters from a Musical Friendship*, edited and translated by Hans Barkan (Norman: University of Oklahoma Press, 1957).

(2) Max Kalbeck's four-volume biography, *Johannes Brahms* (Berlin: Deutsche Brahms-Gesellschaft, 1904–1914; reprinted in 1974 by Schneider in Tutzing).

(3) Margit L. McCorkle and Donald M. McCorkle's catalog of Brahms's works, *Johannes Brahms: thematisch-bibliographisches Werkverzeichnis* (Munich: G. Henle Verlag, 1984).

Presuming that this book will be used principally for reference, I have tried to make each entry complete in itself; some redundancy has been the inevitable result.

It will be apparent too that much of the analysis assumes that a score will be accessible to the reader. A recommended edition is that of Eusebius Mandyczewski, *[Johannes Brahms] Sämtliche Werke* (Leipzig: Breitkopf & Härtel [1926]; reprinted in 1949 by J. W. Edwards in Ann Arbor, Mich.). All of the quartets are found in volume 20, the duets in volume 22. In 1997 the Breitkopf & Härtel *Liebeslieder, Neue Liebeslieder,* and Op. 103 *Zigeunerlieder* were reprinted in one volume by Dover Publications, Inc. C. F. Peters publishes convenient, readable performing editions of all of the duets and quartets except Nos. 1 and 3 of the Op. 75 Ballads and Romances and the

Little Wedding Cantata; I have been unable to locate any source other than the *Sämtliche Werke* for these three pieces, the relevant volumes of the Kalmus Miniature Study Scores being, regrettably, permanently out of print. The Op. 84 Romances and Lieder are published among the solo songs in volume 25 of the Breitkopf & Härtel edition, in Series III of the 1980 Dover reprint, and in volumes 1 (nos. 1, 2, and 4) and 4 (nos. 3 and 5) of the Max Friedländer edition for C. F. Peters.

The layout of the German poetry is that found in the second edition of Gustav Ophüls's *Brahms-Texte: vollständige Sammlung der von Johannes Brahms componirten und musikalisch bearbeiteten Dichtungen* (Berlin: Verlag der Deutschen Brahms-Gesellschaft, 1908); I have modernized the spelling. A recent edition of *Brahms-Texte* by Kristian Wachinger was published in 1983 by Langewiesche-Brandt, Ebenhausen bei München.

The English prose renderings of the song texts are mine, as are translations from sources not published in English. I am grateful to Professor Bernd Kratz of the University of Kentucky German Department for his help with an occasional archaism or opacity.

I would also like to take this opportunity to express my thanks to the administration and voice faculty of the University of Kentucky School of Music for their ongoing encouragement and support.

Brahms's

Vocal Duets and
Quartets with Piano

Introduction

With the publication in 1862 of the Op. 20 duets for soprano and alto, Brahms made his first contribution to the repertoire of *Hausmusik*—music intended for domestic, social use by amateurs.

The tradition of amateur music making was centuries old in German-speaking Europe. The desire of the middle classes to emulate the leisure activities of the aristocracy had led to the founding of the fellowships of mastersingers in the fifteenth century, the remarkable flowering of the part-song in the sixteenth, and the widespread establishment of collegia musica together with the increased popularity of domestic chamber-music playing in the seventeenth century. A typical eighteenth-century German family of some wealth and education enjoyed participating in musical performance at home, partly in order to distance itself from peasants and laborers; singing with one's friends often benefited from instrumental support, and a keyboard instrument became the musical center of many a burgher household. Another outgrowth of the urge for social music making was the *Männerchorvereine* (men's choral societies) that flourished in the early 1800s, followed in due course by mixed choirs and women's choruses. It must be noted, however, that among the circumstances contributing to the popularity of choral singing was the inevitable decline in domestic chamber music as the number of truly competent amateur musicians decreased.

But in Brahms's youth the tradition still flourished, and his first duets followed in the pathway already established by the *Hausmusik* of Schubert, Mendelssohn, and Schumann.

It became evident when the Op. 28 duets appeared a year later that ease of performance was not Brahms's primary consideration but that he was beginning to see his music for concerted solo voices as a parallel to his Lieder composition, with the enhanced possibilities not only for sonority but also for drama and humor that additional voices offered. The emphasis seemed to be shifting from music suitable for amateurs to music intended for social use—there is, after all, a social aspect to the simple act of multiple singers' gathering around the piano.

Though there was certainly still a market for domestic music when the *Liebeslieder* were printed in 1869, Brahms could hardly have been unaware of its erosion. One detects a certain wistfulness in his expression to Simrock of the hope that the waltzes "will become real *Hausmusik,* and will soon be sung a lot" (31 August 1869). It is telling that first performances of the work, both private and public, involved professional musicians. (The group of friends for whom Brahms wrote the *Zigeunerlieder* in the 1880s also included professional musicians.)

In addition to the relatively familiar cycles—the *Liebeslieder, Neue Liebeslieder,* and *Zigeunerlieder*—Brahms composed twenty independent duets, plus the five Romances and Lieder, Op. 84, for one or two voices (here also regarded as duets), and seventeen independent quartets, all for mixed voices. The compositions span the years 1852–1891, a period almost as long as that covered by the solo songs.

Fourteen of the twenty-five duets have texts in the form of dialogues, and they exploit in various ways the drama inherent in that format. Who can remain unmoved by the fateful "Die Nonne und der Ritter," the darkly tragic "Edward," or the terrifying "Walpurgisnacht"? At the other extreme, who can sit unsmiling through the irresistibly good-humored "Der Jäger und sein Liebchen"? Though the early duets barely depart from note-against-note Mendelssohnian thirds and sixths, counterpoint is later used with great mastery for texture contrast, for emphasis, or to suggest dissension or the failure to communicate.

Unlikely as it seems, three of the quartets are also in dialogue form; the scoring is for two male-female pairs in "Wechsellied zum Tanze," separate male and female pairs in "Neckereien," and solo tenor against the other three voices in "Fragen." But generally speaking, Brahms seemed to view the vocal quartet as a sonorously expanded song combined with the linear independence of the string quartet. Certainly a major factor in the enduring pleasure provided by the *Liebeslieder* waltzes, for example, is their chamber-music quality—the ever-changing relationships of counterpoint and timbre among the four voices and four-hand piano.

In his 1911 Brahms biography, Fuller-Maitland could still predict the success of "Fragen" when "a quartet-party has a first-class tenor," but domestic music making dwindled as the twentieth century progressed. Few of us today can think of a single household of non-professional musicians in which scores of the *Liebeslieder* might provide an evening's entertainment. Consequently all of this repertoire except the three large sets is virtually unknown at present because it is performed so rarely, and even those cycles are familiar primarily through the choral performance that Brahms occasionally tolerated but never intended or encouraged.

Many of Brahms's most endearing and imaginative creations are to be found among the vocal duets and quartets. It is time to stop regarding them as a dated, somehow inferior genre and to begin reintroducing them to the public as the treasures they are. They will amply repay acquaintance.

Three Duets
for Soprano and Alto

OPUS 20

Drei Duette für eine Sopran und eine Altstimme mit Begleitung des Pianoforte componirt von Johannes Brahms (Three duets for solo soprano and alto voices with piano accompaniment composed by Johannes Brahms), Op. 20. Published in March 1862 by N. Simrock in Bonn; publication number 6206; German text only.

Brahms spent the summer holiday of 1858 in Göttingen with his recently married friends Julius and Philippine Grimm. There he met and became infatuated with Agathe von Siebold, the dark-haired, sweet-voiced daughter of a medical professor at the university. It is to his delight in her singing that we owe the two "Weg der Liebe" duets of Op. 20, most of the songs of Opp. 14 and 19, and, probably, "Die Schwestern," to be published in 1874 as Op. 61/1. The romance led to an informal engagement and the secret exchange of rings, but, characteristically, Brahms could not bring himself to a firm commitment to marriage. In January 1859 he wrote to her bluntly that, though he loved her, he could not "wear fetters"; anguished, she released him from whatever promises he had made, but with the stipulation that he not return. They never saw each other again.

The Op. 20 duets belong to the long-standing German tradition of *Hausmusik*—pleasant music of no great complexity or difficulty, suitable for performance by amateurs—the most recent noted contributors to which were Mendelssohn and Schumann. Kalbeck, with atypical intolerance, dismisses all three pieces as "routine, Biedermeier products with Mendelssohnian trimmings" and points to their "regular, short-breathed phrasing, schoolmasterly counterpoint, and trivial cadences" (*Johannes Brahms*, I₂, 336).

While it is true that Brahms at twenty-five was not yet the supreme master of text-music synthesis that he was to become, there is much here that is strikingly original and undeniably Brahmsian, given the music's intended audience: the colorful harmonic borrowings from the opposite mode, particularly at cadences; the charming use of contrary motion between the voices and the piano in no. 2; the underlay of heartache in no. 3, which erupts in the wailing lament of the third phrase. Yet the music seems rather to accommodate the text than to embody it, and there is no more than a hint of the terse drama of the vocal writing that is to come.

The nearly constant thirds and sixths have the effect of compressing the two voices into a single, resonance-enhanced entity. Even the contrapuntal contrasts seem rather to intensify the same thought than to produce two distinct identities.

Weg der Liebe, I. Teil, Op. 20/1 (Love's pathway, part I)

Translated from the English by
Johann Gottfried von Herder (1744–1803)

Über die Berge,
   Über die Wellen,
Unter den Gräbern,
   Unter den Quellen,
Über Fluten und See'n,
   In der Abgründe Steg,
Über Felsen, über Höhen,
   Find't Liebe den Weg.

In Ritzen, in Falten,
   Wo der Feu'rwurm nicht liegt,
In Höhlen, in Spalten,
   Wo die Fliege nicht kriecht,
Wo Mücken nicht fliegen
   Und schlüpfen hinweg,
Kommt Liebe, sie wird siegen
   Und finden den Weg!

Sprecht, Amor sei nimmer
   Zu fürchten, das Kind!
Lacht über ihn immer,
   Als Flüchtling, als blind,
Und schließt ihn durch Riegel
   Vom Tag'licht hinweg:
Durch Schlösser und Siegel
   Find't Liebe den Weg.

Wenn Phönix und Adler
   Sich unter euch beugt,

Over the mountains,
   over the waves,
under tombstones,
   under springs,
over floods and seas,
   on a path through the abyss,
over rocks, over heights,
   Love will find the way.

In crevices, in crannies
   where the glowworm cannot lie,
in cavities, in cracks
   where a fly cannot crawl,
where gnats cannot fly
   and expect to escape—
Love will come, it will triumph
   and discover the way!

Declare, Cupid is never
   to be feared, the child!
You may deride him constantly
   as a fugitive, as blind,
and lock him away
   from daylight behind bars:
through locks and seals,
   Love will find the way.

Though phoenix and eagle
   may bend to your will,

Wenn Drache, wenn Tiger	though dragon, though tiger
Gefällig sich neigt,	may bow down obligingly,
Die Löwin läßt kriegen	the lioness may allow you
Den Raub sich hinweg,	to carry away her prey,
Kommt Liebe, sie wird siegen	Love will come, it will triumph
Und finden den Weg.	and discover the way!

E major; $^6_8$; *Allegro;* SA.

Approximate duration: 2′15.

A B C B′ A; the first strophe is repeated at the end to round out a five-part form.

Composed in September 1858, presumably in Göttingen.

A notice in the *Neue Zeitung für Musik* for 6 May 1864 indicates that either Part I or Part II of "Weg der Liebe" was performed in Lucerne on 10 March 1864, the earliest documented public performance. A private performance by Ottilie Ebner-Hauer and Rosa Girzick took place at Theodor Billroth's house on the Alserstrasse in Vienna on 29 January 1878.

The original English poem, "Love Will Find Out the Way," appeared in *Reliques of Ancient English Poetry* (London, 1765) by Thomas Percy (1729–1811). Herder's German translation is found in his *Volkslieder* (Leipzig, 1778–1779), retitled *Stimmen der Völker in Liedern* in 1807. Since "Love Will Find Out the Way" has five verses, it is evident that Herder not only translated but adapted the text, most notably by deriving his third stanza from the combining of stanzas 3 and 4:

> You may esteem him
>   A child for his might;
> Or you may deem him
>   A coward from his flight;
> But if she, whom love doth honour,
>   Be conceal'd from the day,
> Set a thousand guards upon her,
>   Love will find out the way.
>
> Some think to lose him,
>   By having him confin'd;
> And some do suppose him,
>   Poor thing, to be blind;
> But if ne'er so close ye wall him,
>   Do the best that you may,
> Blind love, if so ye call him,
>   Will find out his way.

In Brahms's exuberant setting, the voices, buoyed by the leaping staccato eighths in the accompaniment, quickly soar to a high point in m. 9.
There the bass becomes an octave-doubled line that imitates the opening
vocal motive sequentially through the lowered seventh and lowered sixth
to the dominant, then supports the voices in contrary motion as the harmonies find their way (as surefootedly as the Love of the text) back to the
tonic key to end the section.

Stanza 2 begins with canonic imitation at the unison one measure apart
and modulates to the key of the dominant. The canon seems to have been
motivated more by the desire for contrast than by textual demands, though
the closeness of the imitation may suggest the tightness of the crevices and
crannies, and the mostly stepwise motion, the crawling of the worms and in-
sects.

A brief piano interlude modulates from the dominant B to the key of
G for stanza 3, the lowered-submediant relationship that Brahms so often
associated with imagination or unreality. Some bland counterpoint affords
little contrast because of the rhythmic simultaneity of the voices, but the
passage in octaves at "durch Schlösser und Siegel" is a striking change of
texture.

Stanza 4 is set to a variant of the music for stanza 2, with its canonic
beginning and its modulation, this time from G back to B. The function of
B as dominant of the home tonic is made unmistakable by the change from
G♮ at "Liebe" in m. 89 to G♯ at "siegen" in m. 91.

An exact repetition of the opening strophe rounds out the form and
ends the song. As before, the high A on "Liebe" at the beginning of the concluding phrase provides a satisfying climax, and the insinuation of a C♮ into
the bass line two measures later is a true Brahmsian touch—it both recalls
the lowered-submediant harmonies that are prominent throughout and
adds particular poignancy to the closing repetition of the word "Liebe."

A short postlude, *animato*, based on the canonic melody from strophes
2 and 4, provides a brilliant ending.

Weg der Liebe, II. Teil, Op. 20/2 (Love's pathway, part II)

Translated from the English by
Johann Gottfried von Herder (1744–1803)

Den gordischen Knoten,	Can mortal hand break,
Den Liebe sich band,	can it loosen
Kann brechen, kann lösen	the Gordian knot
Ihn sterbliche Hand?	that Love has tied?
Was müh't ihr, was sinnet	Why trouble yourself, why ponder
Ihr listigen Zweck?	crafty strategy?
Durch was ihr beginnet,	Through whatever you undertake,
Find't Liebe den Weg.	Love will find the way.

Und wär' Er verriegelt,	And if He were imprisoned,
Und wär' Er verkannt,	and if He were unrecognized,
Sein Name versiegelt	His name concealed
Und nimmer genannt,	and never mentioned,
Mitleidige Winde,	sympathetic winds,
Ihr schlüpfet zu mir	you would blow to me
Und brächtet mir Zeitung	and bring me tidings
Und brächtet ihn mir.	and bring him to me.
Wär'st fern über Bergen,	If you were far away over mountains,
Wär'st fern über'm Meer:	if you were far away across the sea,
Ich wandert' durch Berge,	I would walk across mountains,
Ich schwämme durch's Meer;	I would swim across the sea;
Wär'st, Liebchen, ein' Schwalbe	beloved, if you were a swallow
Und schlüpfest am Bach,	gliding at the brook,
Ich, Liebchen, wär' Schwalbe	I'd be a swallow too, darling,
Und schlüpfte dir nach.	and glide after you.

C major; $^6_8$; *Poco Adagio molto espressivo;* SA.

Approximate duration: 2'30.
Strophic.
Composed in September 1858, presumably in Göttingen.

Either Part I or Part II of "Weg der Liebe" was performed in Lucerne on 10 March 1864, according to a notice in the *Neue Zeitschrift für Musik* for 6 May 1864; this was the only documented early performance.

Herder's German translation is found in his *Volkslieder* (Leipzig, 1778–1779), retitled *Stimmen der Völker in Liedern* in 1807. There it is separated from, but seems to be a continuation of, "Weg der Liebe, I. Teil." In fact, Part II does not appear with Part I in Percy's *Reliques of Ancient English Poetry* as many have presumed. An annotation in Herder's index reveals that Part II is from "D'Urfeys [Thomas D'Urfey (1653–1723)] Collection of Songs and Ballads, Vol. 5, p. 34," where it "runs on at considerable length [*steht weitläuftiger*]. Here are only the best strophes."

In verse 3, line 2, Herder wrote "Wär'st weit über'm Meer"; Brahms replaced "weit" with "fern," perhaps for its parallelism with line 1.

The setting is in strong contrast to that of Part I in its quiet intensity, aura of heartfelt personal emotion, harmonic richness, and serene tempo. The voices are rhythmically synchronous throughout except for two passing tones in the alto, and they sing almost entirely in parallel thirds and sixths. All of the phrases are of four measures, including the piano postlude at the end of each strophe. Yet any impression of squareness is minimal because the elegant accompaniment provides continuity and a sense of dramatic progression.

The opening measure establishes quiet motion in constant eighth notes, which continues throughout. The piano's melody moves in contrary motion to that of the voices in phrase 1 and bridges the gap between phrases. In phrase 2 it is the bass line that moves in contrary motion to the voices and doubling piano melody. The left hand's inner voices in phrase 3 move contrary to the right hand; continuing motion in the accompaniment again joins the vocal phrases. The piano melody's attempt at independence from the voices in phrase 3 becomes a reality in phrase 4, and the bass moves in contrary motion to both.

Among the trademark Brahmsian harmonic usages are the early turn to the subdominant (in m. 5) and its minor inflection (in m. 8); the many borrowings from the minor mode, especially in phrase 3 and the postlude; and the chromatic and enharmonic alteration of the diminished seventh in m. 12 into the dominant seventh in m. 13 of the Neapolitan in m. 14— a heightened touch of pathos before the return to the sunny tonic major for the strophe's conclusion.

The lovely postlude seems both to encapsulate and to resolve the preceding drama. Performers should take into account that the interior *fermatas* signal only the ends of strophes rather than full-fledged interruptions of movement.

Since the two parts of "Weg der Liebe" are related only by subject matter and the recurring title phrase, and not by either poetic origin or musical material, there seems not to be the compelling case for pairing them in performance that can be made, for example, for "Scheiden und Meiden" and "In der Ferne," Op. 19/2 and 3, "Sommerabend" and "Mondenschein," Op. 85/1 and 2, or the two parts of "Liebe und Frühling," Op. 3/ 2 and 3. As is also true of "Regenlied" and "Nachklang," Op. 59/3 and 4, each part of "Weg der Liebe" is so complete in itself that in coupling them one risks dilution, rather than enhancement, of their considerable separate effect. (In both cases the objection lessens when the pair is performed in the context of the complete opus.)

Die Meere, Op. 20/3 (The seas)

Text by Wilhelm Müller (1794–1827), after the Italian

Alle Winde schlafen auf dem Spiegel der Flut;	All the winds are asleep on the tide's mirror;
Kühle Schatten des Abends decken die Müden zu.	the cool shadows of evening cover the weary.
Luna hängt sich Schleier über ihr Gesicht,	Luna hangs veils over her face,

Schwebt in dämernden Träumen über die Wasser hin.	hovers over the water in glimmering dreams.
Alles, alles stille auf dem weiten Meer!	Everything, everything is quiet on the broad sea!
Nur mein Herz will nimmer mit zur Ruhe geh'n.	Only my heart refuses to join in the stillness.
In der Liebe Fluten treibt es her und hin,	It is tossed to and fro on torrents of love,
Wo die Stürme nicht ruhen, bis der Nachen sinkt.	where the storms will not abate until the skiff sinks.

E minor; $^6_8$; *Andante;* SA.

Approximate duration: 2'45.

Strophic; the second strophe is extended through repetition of the last line of text.

Composed in April 1860 in Hamburg.

The first public performance was given in Munich on 30 November 1889 by Mathilde von Schelhorn and Marie Schmidtlein with Joseph Giehrl at the piano.

The text is the second of the *Lieder vom Meerbusen von Salerno* in *Lyrische Reisen und epigrammatische Spaziergänge* (1827); it also appears in *Die Volksharfe, Sammlung der schönsten Volkslieder aller Nationen* (Stuttgart, 1838), which was Brahms's source.

The setting is a Mendelssohnian barcarolle—one is reminded of the "Venetianische Gondellieder" from the *Lieder ohne Worte* for piano, Opp. 19/6, 30/6, and 62/5. As in the Mendelssohn models, erotic turmoil and melancholy lurk just below the surface, and mounting tension shatters the placid regularity of phrasing into emotionally charged irregularity as the piece progresses.

At the outset the piano introduces the inexorable rocking motion that will continue to the end. It doubles the tranquil first vocal phrase and continues its melody into the lower octave, spanning the gap between phrases and darkening its doubling of the text's less serene second line. The second phrase acquires an upbeat of two eighths and modulates to the relative major—a signal that change is imminent.

The dramatic crux of both text and music is in the third line. Almost immediately the introduction of a C♯ and A♯ drive the music toward B minor, the A♯ clashing curiously with the A♮ just preceding. The soprano's grace note in m. 14 is like a little sob; the expected four-measure phrase breaks off with a gasp after two, and the second part is extended by a prolonged descending wail, to a total of nearly six measures.

The final phrase, in *pianissimo* contrast to the climactic phrase 3, loses first its C♯, then its A♯, to return to the tonic key. It begins with two eighths before the barline but, since there is no harmonic movement to the downbeat, the effect is rather of an initial three-beat measure than a two-eighth upbeat.

In the second strophe a repetition of the last line of text becomes a codetta in the tonic major, the poet apparently finding some sweetness in the prospect of ceasing to struggle against the torrents of love. The piano, however, doubles darkly in the lower octave as in phrase 2, and the postlude returns sadly to the minor mode.

Four Duets for Alto and Baritone

OPUS 28

Duette für Alt und Bariton mit Begleitung des Pianoforte componirt und Frau Amalie Joachim gewidmet von Johannes Brahms (Duets for alto and baritone with piano accompaniment composed and dedicated to Frau Amalie Joachim by Johannes Brahms), Op. 28. Published in December 1863 by C. A. Spina in Vienna; publication numbers 17,958–61; German only.

The contralto Amalie Joachim (1839–1898), née Schneeweiss, was the wife of the famed Hungarian-born violinist Joseph Joachim (1831–1907), a close friend and leading champion of Brahms. She first gained a reputation in opera under the professional name Weiss but confined her activities to the concert stage after her marriage. She introduced many of Brahms's Lieder and was a renowned interpreter of his Alto Rhapsody; the two songs with viola, Op. 91, were written for her. Brahms sent her the published Op. 28 duets in January 1864 as a belated Christmas gift.

These four duets represent a considerable change in approach from those of Op. 21. All four of the texts are dialogues, almost demanding the treatment of the two voices as separate entities. But the music can tell us more than is possible in the printed poetry. Is there communication or a failure to communicate? Are the viewpoints compatible or opposing? Does the exchange bring the participants closer or drive them apart? Therein lies the drama of the Op. 28 duets.

Die Nonne und der Ritter, Op. 28/1
(The nun and the knight)
Text by Joseph Freiherr von Eichendorff (1788–1857)

Da die Welt zur Ruh' gegangen,

Now that the world has gone to
    sleep,

Wacht mit Sternen mein Verlangen,
In der Kühle muß ich lauschen,
Wie die Wellen unten rauschen!

my longing keeps watch with the stars;
in the coolness, I must listen
to the waves raging below.

"Fernher mich die Wellen tragen,

"I am borne here from afar by the
    waves

Die an's Land so traurig schlagen
Unter deines Fensters Gitter,
Fraue, kennst du noch den Ritter?"

that beat so sadly upon the shore
under your window's lattice—
lady, do you still know your knight?"

Ist's doch, als ob seltsam' Stimmen
Durch die lauen Lüfte schwimmen;
Wieder hat's der Wind genommen,—
Ach, mein Herz ist so beklommen!

It seems as though strange voices
are floating through the balmy air;
the wind has swept them away again—
oh, my heart is so uneasy!

"Drüben liegt dein Schloß verfallen,
Klagend in den öden Hallen,
Aus dem Grund der Wald mich grüßte,

"Yonder lies your ruined castle,
mourning in the abandoned halls;
from its depths the forest greeted
    me—

's war, als ob ich sterben müßte."

it was as if I were destined to die."

Alte Klänge blühend schreiten;
Wie aus lang versunk'nen Zeiten
Will mich Wehmut noch bescheinen,
Und ich möcht' von Herzen weinen.

Old sounds stalk, multiplying;
as from times long buried
melancholy would still envelop me,
and, heart full, I feel like weeping.

"Über'm Walde blitzt's von weitem,

"Beyond the woods, lightning flashes
    from afar,

Wo um Christi Grab sie streiten;

where they are fighting at the tomb of
    Christ.

Dorthin will mein Schiff ich wenden,
Da wird alles, alles enden!"

That is where I will turn my ship;
there everything will end, everything!"

Geht ein Schiff, ein Mann stand
    drinnen,
Falsche Nacht, verwirrst die Sinne!

A ship sets sail, a man stood in it—

deceitful night, you bewilder the
    senses!

Welt Ade! Gott woll' bewahren,
Die noch irr' im Dunkeln fahren!

Farewell world! May God protect those
who still go astray in the darkness!

G minor; $\frac{3}{4}$; *Andante;* AB.

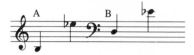

Approximate duration: 5'15.

Varied (double) strophic. Each voice has its own distinctive musical material, but the alto's strophes 3 and 4 are varied, as are the last line of the baritone's strophe 2 and his strophe 3; new accompaniment figures mark each succeeding section.

Composed in November 1860, presumably in Hamburg.

The first public performance was sung (together with that of "Vor der Tür," Op. 28/2) by Ida Flatz and Emil Förchtgott on 18 December 1863 in Vienna.

The poem was written in 1808 and printed in the poet's collected *Gedichte* (Berlin, 1837); Brahms owned the 1843 edition. In the original, line 1 of stanza 6 has "vom weiten," and line 1 of stanza 7, "drinne."

This affecting ballad rises from a quiet beginning to a painful climax as the nun grapples with the past events that haunt her. Only gradually, as details emerge one by one, can the shadowy outlines of the story be inferred. A lady of noble birth has fled to the convent when her knight failed to return from the crusades. In the cool, silent night she is still tormented by longing and overcome by grief. The sound of his voice echoes in her imagination; her last sight of him, standing on the deck of his departing ship, persists in her memory. Finally, as though renewing her vows, she bids farewell to the world, and she prays for God's blessing on those who, like her, waver from their intended course in the deceiving darkness.

The G-minor strophe assigned to the alto features a gently arching shape for phrases 1 and 3 and the half note–quarter note rhythm that is a customary Brahmsian metaphor for isolation. (See, for example, "Anklänge," Op. 7/3; "Herbstgefühl," Op. 48/7; and "Es hing der Reif," Op. 106/3.) The music proceeds in four-measure phrases, the last extended to six measures by an expressive stretching of the penultimate syllable. The sparse accompaniment supports the voice with doleful, archaic-sounding harmonies, one chord per measure.

In its eight-measure interlude, the piano adopts the long-short rhythm and modulates to the relative major.

The music for the baritone, in B♭ major, shares with that of the alto the arching shape for phrases 1 and 3, the half-quarter rhythm, and the four-measure phrase structure, which it retains to the end. The last phrase rises to a passionate outburst and modulates to the dominant of G minor.

A second piano interlude, this one of ten measures, gradually allows the emotional tension to abate in preparation for the nun's resumption of her musing. A new suspension figure is added, causing rhythmic motion on every quarter; this slight increase in activity (in voice and piano combined) underlies the ensuing strophe.

The vocal line of the alto's second strophe exactly repeats that of her first, but the more active rhythm in the accompaniment increases the level of agitation.

The third piano interlude, like the first, modulates to B♭ major for the baritone's strophe, and it introduces a rising broken-chord figure in quarter notes (a variant of the harmonies of the first interlude), a falling version of which accompanies the first two vocal phrases. Restless groups of three eighth notes appear in the left hand as the baritone's third phrase initiates a long crescendo.

The alto's entrance in m. 98, overlapping the baritone's altered last phrase, is a dramatic masterstroke. Not only does the resultant foreshortening markedly raise the emotional level, it also becomes shockingly apparent to the listener that something other than the presumed dialogue is taking place. The opening alto phrase arches a step higher than before, to a clashing dissonance with the baritone at "blühend/sterben" in m. 100, setting the stage for further variation of the strophe. Recollection of past grief divides the third phrase in half with a gasping rest; awareness of approaching tears extends the fourth phrase to eight measures. Eighth notes in the accompaniment are now continuous, divided between the hands in groups of three. The bass pedal E♭ is retained from the baritone's third phrase; its movement in m. 96 sets in motion a harmonic drifting that finally settles in C major (as dominant of F minor) at the *Animato* in m. 111.

Several text repetitions make possible the climactic elaborations of the final portion of the piece. The piano introduces martial-sounding trumpet calls over a rumbling bass in sixteenth notes. The baritone sings his opening arch of melody three times *poco a poco crescendo,* each time a step higher than before. His third line of text is sung to a new phrase alternating the pitches A and C, his fourth line to a near duplicate of the fourth phrase of his original strophe. During this fourth line, the alto again enters unexpectedly to sing the first half of her final strophe—not to her own music, but imitating these two baritone phrases in canon at the seventh. Her last phrase of the section also has the effect of an elongated imitation of the baritone's closing phrase.

The activity winds down; the harmony settles on A as dominant and resolves to D at the *Tempo I.* Softly the nun sings her final prayer to exactly the same music that ended her initial strophe. Two pensive rising arpeggios in quarter notes end the piece in the tonic major.

A noteworthy feature of "Die Nonne und der Ritter" is the restrained use of the piano, which supports the voices, modulates, and varies the dramatic tension, but almost entirely eschews participation in the melodic progress of the piece. The drama itself is thus thrust into prominence, but a piano part that fails to enter into lyric partnership with the voices is a rarity in Brahms's Lieder composition.

Vor der Tür, Op. 28/2 (Outside the door)
Old German Folk Song

Tritt auf den Riegel von der Tür,
Wie gern käm' ich herein
Um dich zu küssen.
"Ich laß' dich nicht herein,
Schleich immer heim ganz sacht
Auf deinen Füßen."

Wohl kann ich schleichen sacht
Wie Mondenschein,
Steh nur auf, laß mich ein;
Das will ich von dir haben,
O Mägdlein, deinen Knaben
Laß ein!

Draw back the bolt from the door,
I want so much to come in
to kiss you.
"I'll not let you in;
steal homeward quite lightly
on your feet."

Indeed, I can creep as softly
as moonlight,
only get up and let me in;
that's what I want from you,
O maiden, let your
lad in!

B major; $\frac{3}{4}$; *Vivace;* AB.

Approximate duration: 2′05.
Through-composed, but resembling a rondo in five sections.
Composed during the winter of 1862, presumably in Vienna.
"Vor der Tür" was first performed in public (as was "Die Nonne und der Ritter," Op. 28/1) by Ida Flatz and Emil Förchtgott on 18 December 1863 in Vienna's Salon Bösendorfer.
Brahms probably took the Old German text from Heinrich Hoffmann von Fallersleben's *Die deutschen Gesellschaftslieder des 16. und 17. Jahrhunderts* (1844).
The setting is a charming, breathlessly paced recreation of a classic situation in German folklore—an insistent swain who begs to be admitted by a maiden who resists his request.
The baritone pleads his case in B major; the alto's refusal begins in B minor but moves through G major, D minor, and D major before concluding in F♯, without a third. Important materials are the lilting curve to which "den Riegel von der Tür" is set in mm. 4–6 (as is the girl's denial, "ich laß' dich nicht herein!" in mm. 26–28) and the yearning motive in rising quarter notes at "wie gern käm' ich herein" in mm. 10–13 (an inexact inversion of which cleverly sets the girl's dismissal, "schleich immer heim ganz sacht," in mm. 32–35).

Though all seems lighthearted, even playful, at the outset, the sighing slurred quarter notes that begin in m. 11 and the chromatic harmonies and increased dissonance that accompany "um dich zu küssen" in mm. 17–24 suggest that genuine ardor prompts the lover's entreaty. The tonal instability of the girl's response reveals an uncertainty that belies the tone of her words; if the accompaniment represents "tittering," as Friedländer speculates (*Brahms's Lieder*, 30), it seems to express unease rather than delight.

In B-major canon, the baritone responds and amplifies his suit while the girl repeats her previous denial (a bit lamely, one feels). But at midstrophe she takes the lead. Each voice rises to the high E for the first time, and E-major and B-major harmonies alternate hypnotically over a B pedal. In m. 62 the B major becomes a dominant seventh, which resolves deceptively at the peak of a four-measure crescendo to C major—the Neapolitan (the key of pathos) in the overall tonic B major and the lowered submediant (the key of desired unreality) in the E major in which we temporarily find ourselves.

From this poignant tonal base, the baritone passionately declares that to be let in is his sole desire; the girl again refuses, helplessly, and the section turns to the dominant of the home key as it ends.

With growing confidence and with emphasis on the tender subdominant, the suitor again pleads his case in the tonic key. Though the girl repeats her refusal, one feels that the two are drawing closer together: the canon is now at the distance of one measure rather than two; her interjections of protest are increasingly ineffectual, as evidenced by their falling pitch in mm. 101–106. In the closing passage beginning at m. 107, her quarter notes rise to D♯, his to E; suddenly he joins her D♯ in m. 114, and the way is paved for the jubilant cadence. The two voices gradually lose their rhythmic independence until they actually coincide at the end, sharing the final word. The piano's ecstatic rising arpeggios span the keyboard in a celebratory conclusion.

This is not the only case in which Brahms seems to tip the scales in favor of the supplicant. The ending is analogous to that of "Willst du, daß ich geh'?" Op. 71/4, where the music strongly implies that the boy has been allowed to stay, or of "Neckereien," Op. 31/2, where the women seem to have been abducted happily despite their protests. In similar vein, Brahms remarked after hearing Hermine Spies sing "Vergebliches Ständchen," Op. 84/4, "In the end, she will let him in, you know!" (Kalbeck, *Johannes Brahms*, III₂, 375).

On the downbeat of m. 22, the Peters edition misprints B for C♯ in the piano bass.

Es rauschet das Wasser, Op. 28/3 (The water rushes)

Text by Johann Wolfgang von Goethe (1749–1832)

Es rauschet das Wasser	The water rushes
Und bleibet nicht stehn;	and is never still;
Gar lustig die Sterne	the stars pass by
Am Himmel hingehn;	quite happily in the heavens;
Gar lustig die Wolken	the clouds stretch out
Am Himmel hinziehn,	quite happily in the heavens:
So rauschet die Liebe	so love rushes
Und fähret dahin.	and travels along.
Es rauschen die Wasser,	The waters rush past,
Die Wolken zergehn;	the clouds disperse;
Doch bleiben die Sterne,	but the stars remain,
Sie wandeln und gehn;	they wander and move;
So auch mit der Liebe,	so it is with love,
Der treuen, geschicht,	true love, the same story—
Sie wegt sich, sie regt sich,	it moves, it stirs,
Und ändert sich nicht.	and never changes.

F major; common time; *In sanfter Bewegung* (with gentle movement); AB.

Approximate duration: 3′25.

A hybrid form in which the two stanzas of text are assigned to the alto and baritone respectively, set to different melodies in the same key; a concluding section repeats both stanzas while combining and developing the two melodies.

Composed 7 May 1862, presumably in Hamburg.

The first public performance (together with that of "Der Jäger und sein Liebchen," Op. 28/4) was sung by Rosa Girzick and Julius Stockhausen in Vienna on 5 March 1869.

The text is from Goethe's Singspiel *Jery und Bätely*. Brahms owned the *Sämmtliche Werke* (Stuttgart, 1860) and *Werke* (Berlin, no date). In the complete works, line 10 has "vergeh'n" and line 12 has "wandeln und steh'n."

The dialogue here is less a difference of opinion than a correction or amplification. The girl speculates that since natural phenomena are mutable, so must love be; the man agrees that all things change but points out that, like the stars, love that is true is also constant.

The piano introduction evolves from canonic imitation of the motive which is to begin the alto's melody and exploits briefly the afterbeats that are to accompany it. It then also announces the beginning of the baritone's melody with its more sustained accompaniment style.

The girl's music has almost the simplicity of a folk song—rhythmically repetitive, solidly tonal two-measure phrases, accompanied by an unadorned afterbeat figure. Only at her repeated fourth couplet are the phrases expanded to three measures and slurred dissonances and chromaticism allowed to creep in. The idea that love may be fleeting is evidently troubling to her—the tonality becomes unstable and veers temporarily into A minor as her melody ends.

The man is portrayed musically as wiser and more sophisticated than the girl. Though he adopts her rhythm, he embellishes it with an elegant little turn; his accompaniment is sonorous and rhythmically varied; when he sings of the constancy of the stars and, later, of love, his common time broadens into $\frac{6}{4}$ meter.

The afterbeat accompaniment returns for the final section but is overwhelmed after three measures by that associated with the baritone melody, *forte*. The alto's first phrase is interrupted by the entrance of the baritone, her second is considerably varied, but her third is nearly intact; the baritone's first three phrases are exactly as before, with yet another turn added. The concluding phrases of both, however, where love is the subject, are elaborated and extended through text repetition into a culminating section of eight measures; the original basic shapes and defining pitches of both remain recognizable. Championing love's steadfastness, the baritone alone has the last word, sweeping aside the alto's lingering A-minor concern with a reassuring flood of movement toward the tonic F.

As postlude, the piano repeats the music of the introduction in its entirety, adding two measures of plagal-cadenced benediction. The accompaniment bass note on the second half of the first downbeat should be F, as in the introduction; Peters misprints a G.

Der Jäger und sein Liebchen, Op. 28/4
(The hunter and his sweetheart)
Text by August Heinrich Hoffmann von Fallersleben (1798–1874)

Ist nicht der Himmel so blau?
Steh' am Fenster und schau'!
   Erst in der Nacht,
   Spät in der Nacht
Komm' ich heim von der Jagd.

Mädchen, der Himmel ist blau,
Bleib' am Fenster und schau',

Is not the sky so blue?
Stand by the window and watch!
   Not until night,
   Late at night,
will I come home from the hunt.

Maiden, the sky is blue,
wait by the window and watch,

Bis in der Nacht,	until in the night,
Spät in der Nacht	late at night,
Heim ich kehr' von der Jagd.	I return home from the hunt.
"Anders hab' ich gedacht,	"I had other plans,
Tanzen will ich die Nacht!	I want to go dancing tonight!
Bleib' vor der Tür,	Stay outside the door,
Spät vor der Tür	late outside the door,
Willst du nicht tanzen mit mir!"	if you don't want to dance with me!
"Ist auch der Himmel so blau,	"However blue the sky may be,
Steh' ich doch nimmer und schau'	I still will not stand and watch
Ob in der Nacht,	whether in the night,
Spät in der Nacht	late at night,
Heim du kehrst von der Jagd."	you return home from the hunt."

F major; $\frac{2}{4}$; *Allegro;* AB.

Approximate duration: 1′20.

Varied strophic.

Composed in November 1860, presumably in Hamburg.

Rosa Girzick and Julius Stockhausen sang the first public performance (together with that of "Es rauschet das Wasser," Op. 28/3) at a Brahms-Stockhausen concert in Vienna on 5 March 1869.

The text is from the poet's *Lieder und Romanzen* (Cologne, 1821). It appears also in the Leipzig complete editions of 1834 and 1843 but is missing from later editions. Hoffmann wrote, in verse 1, "Heim ich komm' von der Jagd" and, in verse 4, "Heim du kommst von der Jagd."

Brahms's setting is a spirited perpetual motion, a delight for performers and listeners alike. The hunter and his sweetheart are at cross-purposes at the beginning and remain so at the end; in the entire song they sing together only the cadence in mm. 69–71, where the text is "von der Jagd," the exact cause of the dissension.

The embellished dominant-tonic cadence figure that serves as an introduction is an important structural element and will be referred to hereafter as "motive *x.*"

The baritone's initial strophe is evocative of folk song, with its triad- and scale-based melody and its avoidance of modulation. It comprises a repeated three-measure upward-spiraling phrase, two two-measure descending phrases, and a climactic five-measure scalar ascent and descent. The left hand of the accompaniment doubles the two pairs of phrases, with slight variation in mm. 5 and 8 and some connecting melodic movement to bridge the vocal rests. At the scalar climax, however, the piano invents a melodic motive in sixths that falls, in contrary motion to the voice's rising line; as the voice descends, the piano's bass begins a canonic imitation of the entire phrase. The descending half extends into the interlude, where it is accompanied by the right hand's imitation of the ascent; both the ascent and descent are extended into the next octave, forming a punctuating codetta to the strophe.

A statement of motive *x* modulates to the key of the subdominant for the alto's variant strophe. The phrase structure is unchanged, but an interior deviation reduces the compass of the repeated three-measure phrase from a sixth to a fourth; the left hand of the accompaniment is as before (though transposed), but the right introduces a new figure in slurred sixteenths, somewhat moderating the prevailing jauntiness. The alto's two-measure phrase (in G minor) is repeated rather than continuing downward, and the baritone imitates in canon at the seventh. The five-measure scalar phrase is in D minor and its shape is a rough inversion of the original; it begins with a short descent and ascent, which the baritone and piano imitate in canon as the alto concludes with a long rising line. Three statements of motive *x* modulate to G major, to C major, and to F for the final strophe.

The alto sings the first ten measures of the original melody; the baritone imitates the two three-measure phrases contrapuntally, the two two-measure phrases in canon at the fourth. There is then inserted a long, modulatory development before the recurrence of the closing scalar phrase.

Beginning in m. 53, two variant versions of motive *x* modulate to D♭ and D, and an unvaried statement moves to an important cadence on G.

Among the most striking passages in this continually arresting duet is that beginning in m. 63, where first the baritone, then the alto, has eight measures of sustained quarter notes amid the general hustle and bustle of staccato eighths with afterbeats. The baritone's rising-triad figure arrives at E♭ major, F major, and G minor and moves on to a cadence in F; the alto's marks G♭ major, A♭ major, and B♭ minor, from which there is movement through the Neapolitan to a dominant-tonic cadence in F. This four-chord cadence formula is reiterated twice more, and suddenly, like the return of a long-absent friend, the strophe's postponed scalar final phrase appears in the alto voice.

As she sings the ascent, the baritone has the pitches of the descent; as she sings the descent, the baritone and piano begin the canonic imitation of the whole phrase that the piano alone had in strophe 1. As before, the descending half extends beyond the strophe proper, a metaphor for the couple's failure to agree. Again the right hand accompanies with the melody of the ascent, and again both are extended into the next octave. The whole pattern forms a brilliant finale, not only to the strophe but also to the entire piece and opus.

Three Quartets

OPUS 31

Drei Quartette für vier Solostimmen (Sopran, Alt, Tenor, und Bass) mit Pianoforte componirt von Johannes Brahms (Three quartets for four solo voices [soprano, alto, tenor, and bass] with piano composed by Johannes Brahms), Op. 31. Published in three booklets in July 1864 by Breitkopf & Härtel in Leipzig; publication numbers 10639–41; German texts only.

The three quartets exemplify several aspects of Brahms's understanding of the medium. "Wechsellied zum Tanze" is a dialogue between groups of both genders, and "Neckereien" is a male-female exchange with implications of universality; the mixed-voice quartet divides itself naturally into male-plus-female or male-versus-female pairs, as needed, to become an expanded duet, at the same time enriching the dramatic possibilities inherent in the dialogue format. "Der Gang zum Liebchen," on the other hand, is the expression of a single persona, and the setting combines characteristics of a sonority-enhanced solo song with those of the string quartet. The refined part-writing and exploitation of color that are typical of chamber music are hallmarks of Brahms's composition for accompanied vocal quartet.

Wechsellied zum Tanze, Op. 31/1
(Dialogue song at the dance)
Text by Johann Wolfgang von Goethe (1749–1832)

Die Gleichgültigen	*The indifferent ones*
Komm' mit, o Schöne, komm' mit mir zum Tanze;	Come along, O fair one, come with me to the dance;
Tanzen gehöret zum festlichen Tag.	to dance befits a festival day.

Bist du mein Schatz nicht, so kannst du
es werden,
Wirst du es nimmer, so tanzen wir
doch.
Komm' mit, o Schöne, komm' mit mir
zum Tanze;
Tanzen gehöret zum festlichen Tag.

Die Zärtlichen
Ohne dich, Liebste, was wären die
Feste?
Ohne dich, Süße, was wäre der Tanz?

Wärst du mein Schatz nicht, so möcht'
ich nicht tanzen,
Bleibst du es immer, ist Leben ein Fest.

Ohne dich, Liebste, was wären die
Feste?
Ohne dich, Süße, was wäre der Tanz?

Die Gleichgültigen
Laß sie nur lieben, und laß du uns
tanzen!
Schmachtende Liebe vermeidet den
Tanz.
Schlingen wir fröhlich den drehenden
Reihen,
Schleichen die andern zum däm-
mernden Wald.
Laß sie nur lieben, und laß du uns
tanzen,
Schmachtende Liebe vermeidet den
Tanz.

Die Zärtlichen
Laß sie sich drehen und laß du uns
wandeln!
Wandeln der Liebe ist himmlischer
Tanz.
Amor, der nahe, der höret sie spotten,
Rächet sich einmal und rächet sich
bald.
Laß sie sich drehen und laß du uns
wandeln,
Wandeln der Liebe ist himmlischer
Tanz.

If you're not my sweetheart, you can
become so;
if you never do, we can dance anyway.

Come along, O fair one, come with me
to the dance;
to dance befits a festival day.

The amorous ones
Without you, dearest, what would
holidays be?
Without you, sweet one, what would
dancing be?
If you were not my sweetheart, I would
not want to dance;
if you always will be, life will be a
holiday.
Without you, dearest, what would
holidays be?
Without you, sweet one, what would
dancing be?

The indifferent ones
Just leave them to their loving, and
let's dance!
Languishing love shuns dancing.

While we merrily twirl in circling lines,

the others will sneak off to the dimly lit
woods.
Just leave them to their loving, and let's
dance!
Languishing love shuns dancing.

The amorous ones
Let them twirl, and let's go strolling!

The strolling of love is heavenly dance.

Cupid, nearby, hears them mocking;
he'll avenge himself once, and avenge
himself soon.
Let them twirl, and let's go strolling!

The strolling of love is heavenly dance.

C minor/A♭ major; $\frac{3}{4}$; *Tempo di Menuetto, con moto;* SATB.

Approximate duration: 5′45.

Minuet and trio, enlarged by the recurrence of the trio and the addition of a coda.

Composed in November 1859 in Detmold.

The first public performance was sung (from manuscript) on 18 December 1863 at the Salon Bösendorfer in Vienna by Ottilie Hauer, Ida Flatz, Eduard Tisch, and Emil Förchtgott.

The text is from volume 1, *Lieder*, of Goethe's *Gedichte*. Brahms owned the *Sämmtliche Werke* (Stuttgart, 1860) and *Werke* (Berlin, no date).

Against a background of dance music, Brahms sets the dialogue for two male-female pairs—alto and bass as the indifferent couple, soprano and tenor as the amorous ones. The former extol the pleasures of the dance to a stylized, formal minuet in C minor, in vocal lines filled with ungraceful leaps and in awkward, inexact imitation; to increasingly *Ländler*-like music in Ab major, the latter champion lovemaking instead, their fluid, simultaneous vocal lines replete with stepwise movement and yearning appoggiaturas.

Both minuet and trio are in the standard binary form, although the double statement of the minuet's first eight measures (supplied by the piano introduction to stanza 1) is lacking in its reappearance for stanza 3 of the text. The coda repeats lines 1 and 2 of stanzas 3 and 4 while juxtaposing and developing musical elements from both earlier sections. Modulatory, it begins in Ab minor and works its way (twice) through Cb major, E major, and Eb major to Ab major, the key of the amorous couple, to end. Though never withdrawing from their stated position, the indifferent ones seem to be drawn closer to the opposite viewpoint (perhaps prompted by their own suggestion, "If you're not my sweetheart, you can become so"). Besides adopting the other key, they now sing together rather than in imitation and, after a spirited exchange in short phrases, join their counterparts in a full-fledged quartet for the closing period; there also the characteristics of the *Ländler* melody seem to be reconciled with the bass rhythm of the minuet.

Many have remarked upon the anticipatory resemblance in character of the "Wechsellied" to the *Liebeslieder* waltzes. Many too have attributed its Schubertian aura to the influence of Brahms's diligent study of earlier music during his employment by the court at Detmold, Kalbeck even going so far as to cite the first part of the trio as "one of the few works of Brahms that refers to Mozart" (*Johannes Brahms*, I₂, 396). Whatever its origins, the grace and charm of the piece are undeniable. Its imaginative use of the four voices and piano to heighten the drama inherent in Goethe's dialogue is a harbinger of the mastery to come.

Neckereien, Op. 31/2 (Banter)

Translated from the Moravian by Joseph Wenzig (1807–1876)

Fürwahr, mein Liebchen, ich will
nun frei'n,
Ich führ' als Weibchen dich bei mir
ein,
Mein wirst du, o Liebchen, fürwahr du
wirst mein,
Und wolltest du's auch nicht sein.

"So werd' ich ein Täubchen von
weißer Gestalt,
Ich will schon entfliehen, ich flieg' in
den Wald,
Mag dennoch nicht Deine, mag
dennoch nicht dein,
Nicht eine Stunde sein."

Ich hab' wohl ein Flintchen, das trifft
gar bald,
Ich schieß' mir das Täubchen herunter
im Wald;
Mein wirst du, o Liebchen, fürwahr du
wirst mein,
Und wolltest du's auch nicht sein.

"So werd' ich ein Fischchen, ein
goldener Fisch,
Ich will schon entspringen in's Wasser
frisch;
Mag dennoch nicht Deine, mag
dennoch nicht dein,
Nicht eine Stunde sein."

Ich hab' wohl ein Netzchen, das
fischt gar gut,
Ich fang' mir den goldenen Fish in
der Flut;
Mein wirst du, o Liebchen, fürwahr du
wirst mein,
Und wolltest du's auch nicht sein.

"So werd' ich ein Häschen voll
Schnelligkeit,
Und lauf' in die Felder, die Felder
breit,
Mag dennoch nicht Deine, mag
dennoch nicht dein,
Auch nicht eine Stunde sein."

Truly, my darling, I want to go
a-courting now,
I'll set you up as my little wife;
mine you'll be, my pet, indeed you'll
be mine,
even if you don't want to be.

"Then I'll become a little white-
feathered dove,
indeed I'll escape, I'll fly into the
woods;
I don't want to be yours, don't want to
be yours,
not for a single hour."

Indeed I have a little musket that
fires right away,
I'll shoot myself the little dove down in
the woods;
mine you'll be, my pet, indeed you'll
be mine,
even if you don't want to be.

"Then I'll become a little fish, a
golden fish,
indeed I'll escape into the fresh water.

I don't want to be yours, don't want to
be yours,
not for a single hour."

Indeed I have a little net that fishes
very well,
I'll capture myself the golden fish in
the stream;
mine you'll be, my pet, indeed you'll
be mine,
even if you don't want to be.

"Then I'll become a little hare, quick
as a flash,
and run into the fields, the wide fields,

I don't want to be yours, don't want to
be yours,
not even for a single hour."

Ich hab' wohl ein Hündchen, gar pfiffig und fein,	Indeed I have a little hound, very cunning and fine,
Das fängt mir das Häschen im Felde schon ein;	that will surely catch me the little hare in the field;
Mein wirst du, o Liebchen, fürwahr du wirst mein,	mine you'll be, my pet, indeed you'll be mine,
Und wolltest du's auch nicht sein.	even if you don't want to be.

E major; common time; *Allegretto con grazia;* SATB.

Approximate duration: 2'20.

A B A B A'.

Composed 24 December 1863 in Vienna.

The first public performance was sung from manuscript (together with "Wechsellied zum Tanze," Op. 31/1) by Ottilie Hauer, Ida Flatz, Eduard Tisch, and Dr. Kotschy on 11 January 1864 in Vienna at a concert for the benefit of the *Singakademie.* The same two quartets were sung on 17 April 1864 (from manuscript or printer's proofs) at an all-Brahms concert in Vienna's Musikvereinssaal by Marie Wilt, Ida Flatz, F. Prihoda, and Dr. Panzer.

The text is from *Slawische Volkslieder* (Halle, 1830); Brahms probably used the later edition which he owned, *Westslawischer Märchenschatz* (Leipzig, 1857).

The verbal battle takes place in two tonal domains, already defined by the piano's tiny introduction: the men declare their intention to carry the women home as their wives in the tonic, E major; the women inhabit the dominant, B major, where they voice their objections.

Stanza 1 is fugal. The tenor states the angular subject and proceeds with a more coaxing countersubject against the bass's tonal answer. A single secondary dominant introduces the authentic cadence of the otherwise completely diatonic section.

The women sing stanza 2 to more graceful music in the dominant, their lines simultaneous rather than contrapuntal. Their "I don't want to be yours" in m. 21 rises to a vehement *forte,* but their accompaniment shows signs of weakness—it continues the beat-afterbeat pattern from stanza 1, but beats 2 and 4 are missing.

Daringly, the men enter the women's tonal area and interrupt, usurping the women's tune but altering it to return to the tonic, where their own music now begins in canon (m. 29).

The same process is repeated for stanza 4 and the first half of stanza 5, but with the return of the men's key and music in m. 51 (*Animato*) a free-for-all breaks out.

The music is a variation of the men's E-major opening, but the four voices are contrapuntally independent. The text is stanza 6 for the women, but the end of stanza 5 and stanza 7 for the men. The principal subject returns in (slightly altered) canon as expected in m. 51, but astonishingly it appears also in the tonic key in the soprano part in m. 55, trailed by the alto in pseudocanon in mm. 56–57. As though recognizing that the women are now in their territory and borrowing their identity, in m. 59 the men seem to set out deliberately to entice the women into participating in a full authentic cadence in E major—the ultimate conquest. Accordingly they embark upon a development of the earlier coaxing countersubject stressing the subdominant, in effect obliterating the women's tonal area with their A-major harmonies and their D♯s. Protesting to the end, the women happily capitulate, and the piano propels the piece to a celebratory conclusion.

The ease with which the women are bested, their rather formulaic protestation, and indeed, the title suggest that the whole exchange has been more a game than an actual conflict. In any case, the piece is a delight, a charming representation of the eternal battle of the sexes.

Der Gang zum Liebchen, Op. 31/3 (Going to his sweetheart)

Translated from the Bohemian by Joseph Wenzig (1807–1876)

Es glänzt der Mond nieder,	The moon is shining down;
Ich sollte doch wieder	I really should return
Zu meinem Liebchen,	to my sweetheart,
Wie mag es ihr geh'n?	to see how she is doing.
Ach weh', sie verzaget	Alas, she is despondent
Und klaget, und klaget,	and laments, and laments,
Daß sie mich nimmer	that she will never see me
Im Leben wird seh'n!	again in this life!
Es ging der Mond unter,	The moon set;
Ich eilte doch munter,	I hurried quite briskly,
Und eilte, daß keiner	and hurried so nobody might
Mein Liebchen entführt.	carry my sweetheart away.
Ihr Täubchen, o girret,	Oh, coo, little doves;
Ihr Lüftchen, o schwirret,	oh, hum, little breezes,
Daß keiner mein Liebchen,	that no one might carry my sweetheart,
Mein Liebchen entführt!	my sweetheart away!

E♭ major; $\frac{3}{4}$; *Con moto e grazioso;* SATB.

Approximate duration: 2′50.

Strophic, with coda.

Composed on Christmas eve 1863 in Vienna.

The first public performance was given in Karlsruhe on 3 November 1865 by Fräulein Wabel, Frau Hauser, Herr Stolzenberg, and Herr Hauser.

The text, like that of the preceding quartet, is found in Wenzig's *Slawische Volkslieder* (Halle, 1830) and the later edition, *Westslawischer Märchenschatz* (Leipzig, 1857). Brahms also set the poem to different music as a solo song, Op. 48/1.

The present version uses the same music as the fifth of the Op. 39 waltzes for piano or piano duet, including its inner-voice melody at the beginning and its two-measure addition at the end to the prevailing four-measure phrase structure. The homophonic vocal texture reflects the first person singular of the text ("Ich sollte doch wieder zu meinem Liebchen"), and its solidity creates a suitable air of finality for the closing number in the opus.

In contrast to the aura of anxiety that suffuses the solo setting, various elements combine here to create an overriding sense of solicitous tenderness. Among them are the long, lyric piano introduction that returns enlarged as postlude; the many passages with parallel sixths or tenths between voices, for example, soprano and bass in mm. 9–10, alto and bass in mm. 10–12, and soprano and bass in mm. 13–14; the occasional minor tinges in a nonmodulating context, as at the end of the introduction, the dissonance marking "Ach weh'" in m. 17, and the inflected plagal final cadence; and the numerous downbeat suspensions—particularly effective is the contrasting material at mm. 17–20 with its simultaneous pairs of parallel voices and its double suspensions.

In a letter of 25 June 1865 to the music critic Adolf Schubring, Brahms characterized "Der Gang zum Liebchen" as "a pleasant waltz of middling tempo"; obviously the *con moto* instruction is meant to be moderated to accommodate the eighth-note motion of the accompaniment.

Liebeslieder

OPUS 52 (SONGS OF LOVE)

TRANSLATED FROM VARIOUS LANGUAGES
BY GEORG FRIEDRICH DAUMER (1800–1875)

*Liebeslieder. Walzer für das Pianoforte zu vier Händen (und Gesang ad libitum) com-
ponirt von Johannes Brahms* (Songs of love. Waltzes for piano, four hands,
[and optional voices] composed by Johannes Brahms), Op. 52. Published
in October 1869 by N. Simrock in Berlin; publication number 364; German only. A version for piano duet without voices, Op. 52a, appeared in
December 1874 (publication number 7523), and one for voices with piano
solo in April/May 1875 (publication number 7522). At the request of the
conductor Ernst Rudorff, Brahms arranged a suite of *Liebeslieder* for SATB
soli or chorus with small orchestra during the winter of 1869/70, which was
first published only in 1938 by C. F. Peters in Leipzig; publication numbers
11392 (score) and 11397 (parts); it comprised Op. 52/1, 2, 4, 6, 5; a new
number to be published later as Op. 65/9; and Op. 52/11, 8, 9.

The work may have been conceived as early as July 1868 but was completed in August 1869 in Lichtental near Baden-Baden. Clara Schumann
wrote in her diary on 16 July 1869:

> At the beginning of this month Johannes brought me some charming wal-
> tzes for four hands and four voices, sometimes two and two, sometimes all
> four together, with very pretty words, chiefly of the folk-song type....
> They are extraordinarily attractive (charming even without the voices)
> and I very much enjoy playing them.

And on 24 August:

> I went to Karlsruhe to hear Johannes's waltzes with the vocal parts sung by
> Fräulein Murjohn, the Hausers, and Herr Stolzenberg. It was a very great

treat. They are delightfully dainty and charming, of really remarkable musical form and melody.

The first public performance of the complete work took place on 5 January 1870 in the Kleiner Redoutensaal in Vienna. The singers were Luise Dustmann, Rosa Girzick, Gustav Walter, and Emil Krauss; the pianists, Clara Schumann and Brahms. Partial performances, private hearings, and open rehearsals had occurred during the preceding several months in Vienna and Karlsruhe. The version without voices, Op. 52a, was first performed on 14 November 1874 in Vienna by Brahms and Otto Dessoff. The suite for voices and orchestra had its first performance in Berlin on 19 March 1870, with Anna von Asten, Amalie Joachim, Herr Borchardt, Herr Putsch, and the orchestra of the Berlin Hochschule, Ernst Rudorff conducting.

The texts are from *Polydora, ein weltpoetisches Liederbuch* (Frankfurt am Main, 1855).

Both the title and the performance medium of the work had a precedent in Robert Schumann's *Spanische Liebeslieder,* Op. 138, composed in 1849 and published in 1857.

Through the work of Joseph Lanner and the two Johann Strausses, the Viennese waltz had become a large-scale orchestral composition intended for public performance, consisting of several dances with an introduction and a coda, and transitional material where necessary. Brahms's model, however, was rather the smaller German dances and *Ländler* of Schubert, written for piano and for more intimate performance, and comprising series of brief separate dances without additional material. Brahms was a great admirer of Schubert's music and an enthusiastic collector of Schubert manuscripts. In fact, a collection of twenty *Ländler* that Brahms had selected from his store of unpublished Schubert autographs, arranged as a coherent whole and edited anonymously, appeared in print in May 1869, about the time he was leaving for the summer in Lichtental.

Although the composition of the various waltzes of the *Liebeslieder* seems to have gone quickly, their ordering and format (and even their title) proved troublesome. When Brahms sent them to Simrock for publication, he wrote (28 August 1869):

> I am a little uncertain about the title and the division into parts (*Heftordnung*). You can eliminate "Liebeslieder." Do you prefer "Waltzes" for Piano Duet and in parentheses (with voices) or (voices *ad lib.*)? . . .
>
> I should think two booklets with nine each?
>
> It also works well in one volume? Or do you want to make three booklets of six each? In that case, I would ask that numbers 7–12 be arranged as follows: 10, 11, 12, 7, 8, 9. (*Briefwechsel,* IX, 76; my translation)

Still undecided, he suggested to Hermann Levi shortly before the performance that Levi was preparing for 6 October in Karlsruhe that he perform the waltzes in two parts, the first comprising nos. 1–6 and 10–12; the second, nos. 7–9 and 13–18. (Only ten of the eighteen were actually performed in Karlsruhe.) There were other changes right up to publication and beyond—in his own copy of the first edition Brahms indicated that no. 3, "O die Frauen," should be in A major rather than B♭ major, undeniably making a smoother progression of keys. It seems clear that Brahms's goal was the creation of large subgroupings within a coherent whole.

In the work as published, nos. 1–6 constitute the first group. The keys flow logically because of their relatedness to A as a center, and the larger-scale no. 6 functions as a conclusion, its interior section in F major even clarifying the kinship of no. 4 in the same key.

The second group comprises nos. 7–9, whose keys descend by thirds to the E major in which the work began. The initial A♭ of no. 7, which is the tonic of no. 8, is enharmonically the related G♯; there is an important movement into A major in the second half of no. 7 and an analogous movement into E major in no. 8. Brahms obviously considered no. 9 an ending piece since he not only positioned it to conclude the first half of the work but also chose it to end the orchestrated suite and the second group of six if the work were divided into thirds.

Nos. 10–12 lead harmonically one to the next and share the rhythmic motive of a dotted quarter plus three eighth notes; in fact they appear together in the same order in the autograph, on paper of a different type from that of their neighbors.

The A♭ major of no. 13 relates easily to the E♭ major of no. 12, and indeed key signatures of three, four, or five flats lead forward to the end. The ending of no. 18 is elaborated to allow it to function as a conclusion for the set. The enharmonic change of its second half from D♭ major to C♯ major (and the E-major and A-minor harmonies that are initially prominent there) may be intended to relate the end of the work visually to its beginning.

But there was yet another publication problem. Simrock, fearing that the inclusion of a vocal quartet would hamper sales, wanted to issue the version for piano duet alone at the same time, but Brahms insisted that it be delayed (31 August 1869):

> The waltzes will have to appear just the way they stand. Whoever wants to play them without the voices will have to read them from the score. Under no circumstances may they be printed for the first time without the voice parts. This is how they must be brought before the public eye. And let us hope that they will become real *Hausmusik* and will soon be sung a lot. (*Briefwechsel*, IX, 80; Eng. trans. in Gál, *Johannes Brahms*, trans. Stein, p. 179)

The indication "voices *ad libitum*" is a compromise which, to Brahms's regret, became the source of considerable confusion.

In a rare expression of self-satisfaction, Brahms, when returning the corrected proofs to Simrock, remarked that it was the first time that seeing one of his own works in print had brought a smile to his face. "I'll risk being called a jackass if our *Liebeslieder* don't bring joy to some people" (5 October 1869). (*Briefwechsel*, IX, 85; my translation).

The *Liebeslieder* waltzes quickly became popular, as Brahms had hoped, and together with the Hungarian Dances brought their composer international fame and considerable wealth. Their Viennese lilt is occasionally tinged with a gypsy flavor. All of the dances are in $\frac{3}{4}$ meter. The indication *Im Ländler-Tempo* stands for the work as a whole. In that regard, Brahms's instruction to Ernst Rudorff is significant (2 February 1870):

> I don't need to tell you that the tempo of the *Ländler* is moderate. Especially the livelier ones [should be] moderate (C minor, A minor), the more sentimental ones please not dragging ("Hopvine"). (*Briefwechsel*, III, 156; my translation)

Approximate duration of the entire cycle: 23′30.

1.

Russian

Rede, Mädchen, allzu liebes,	Tell me, maiden, all too dear,
Das mir in die Brust, die kühle,	who by your glances have roused
Hat geschleudert mit dem Blicke	in my breast, my cool breast,
Diese wilden Glutgefühle!	these wild feelings of passion!
Willst du nicht dein Herz erweichen,	Will you not soften your heart?
Willst du, eine Überfromme,	Do you want to remain,
Rasten ohne traute Wonne,	nunlike, without the joy of rapture,
Oder willst du, daß ich komme?	or do you want me to come to you?
Rasten ohne traute Wonne—	To remain without the joy of rapture—
Nicht so bitter will ich büßen.	I will not pay such a bitter penalty.
Komme nur, du schwarzes Auge,	Just come to me, you of the dark eyes,
Komme, wenn die Sterne grüßen.	come when the stars appear.

E major; *Im Ländler-Tempo;* SATB.

Approximate duration: 1′20.
Rounded binary; A A′ B A″ B′ A‴ codetta.

Appropriately, the first two stanzas of text are set for the paired male voices, while the maiden's response in stanza 3 is given to the female voices. The four voices sing together only at the end, where the men, as though disbelieving their good fortune, three times repeat their question from verse 2, "Willst du, daß ich komme?"

Over a conventional waltz accompaniment, a prominent appoggiatura figure appears at the outset in the tenor part and in the right hands of both pianists, immediately establishing the caressing tone that pervades much of the set. The figure is freely inverted in the varied returns at the ends of stanzas 2 and 3. Also important thematically is the eighth-note changing-tone figure in the left hand of the *primo* pianist, which lends its rhythm to the cadences of the A section and is also freely inverted in the varied returns.

The young man refers to his customary coolness wholly in the tonic key, but mention of the passion aroused by the maiden's gaze prompts a cadence in the mediant. Both the reference to nunlike behavior in verse 2 and the rejection of that behavior as too bitter a penance in verse 3 are accompanied by a transient modulation to the lowered submediant, whose foreign sound Brahms often called upon to suggest those things imagined or untrue. The codetta features antiphonal free imitations of the final cadence, alternating between the female voices doubled by the piano *primo* and the male voices with the piano *secondo*.

2.

Russian-Polish Dance Song

Am Gesteine rauscht die Flut,	The torrent breaks against the rocks,
Heftig angetrieben:	violently driven.
Wer da nicht zu seufzen weiß,	He who does not know how to sigh
Lernt es unterm Lieben.	will learn to from loving.

A minor; SATB.

Approximate duration: 0′45.
Binary.
The initial upbeats of the piano *primo* make unmistakable the dominant-tonic relationship of the preceding waltz to this.

A predominant feature is the nearly constant use of hemiola, not always simultaneously—in the second four-measure phrase the soprano begins a hemiola pattern a measure later than the tenor and piano *primo*.

The *secondo* is nearly always in conflict with the hemiola; its afterbeats and frequent second-beat neighboring tones in the bass also contribute to the general agitation.

3·
Russian-Polish Dance Song

O die Frauen, o die Frauen,	Oh, women, oh, women,
Wie sie Wonne tauen!	how they spread delight!
Wäre lang ein Mönch geworden,	I would have become a monk long ago,
Wären nicht die Frauen!	were it not for women!

B♭ or A major; TB.

Approximate duration: 1′15.
Binary.
In his editorial comment for the Breitkopf & Härtel edition, Mandyczewski notes that Brahms indicated in his own copy of the first edition that "O die Frauen" should be in A major, presumably finding the key progression smoother. Accordingly, that edition prints it in both keys—no. 3a in A, no. 3b in B♭. The transposition to A major is recommended.
The easy transition from the A minor of no. 2 to A major combines with the less complex rhythm of no. 3 to create a markedly quieter mood, to which the reduction to two voices also contributes. The freely sequential construction of the first two phrases of the second part recalls the analogous situation in no. 2. "Wonne" in the first part and "wären nicht die Frauen" in the second elicit richly colored harmonies.
In m. 6 of the piano *secondo* bass, Mandyczewski chooses the reading G-D (F♯-C♯ in A major) from the manuscript rather than the repetition of m. 5, B♭-D (A-C♯), as in the first edition.

4·
Russian-Polish Dance Song

Wie des Abends schöne Röte	I, poor lass, would like to glow
Möcht' ich arme Dirne glüh'n,	like the lovely red of evening,
Einem, Einem zu gefallen,	to please someone, someone,
Sonder Ende Wonne sprüh'n.	to disperse rapture endlessly.

F major; SA.

Approximate duration: 0′50.
Binary.

F major relates to the preceding A major as the lowered submediant, Brahms's favored tonal area for the hypothetical. The kinship with A is further defined by its initial prominence as a melodic pitch and by the movement to A minor for the cadence of the first part.

The scoring for female voices balances the male-voice pairing of no. 3. The many downbeat appoggiatura chords yearn touchingly.

5.
Russian

Die grüne Hopfenranke,	The green hopvine
Sie schlängelt auf der Erde hin.	trails along the ground.
Die junge, schöne Dirne,	The young, beautiful girl
So traurig ist ihr Sinn!	is so filled with sadness!
Du höre, grüne Ranke!	Listen, green vine!
Was hebst du dich nicht himmelwärts?	Why don't you climb heavenward?
Du höre, schöne Dirne!	Listen, pretty girl!
Was ist so schwer dein Herz?	Why is your heart so heavy?
Wie höbe sich die Ranke,	How could the vine climb
Der keine Stütze Kraft verleiht?	when no pole lends its support?
Wie wäre die Dirne fröhlich,	How could the girl be happy
Wenn ihr der Liebste weit?	when her beloved is far away?

A minor; SATB.

Approximate duration: 1′45.
Binary.

The use here of the paired voices in alternation (only the last two lines of text are sung by the entire quartet) and the return of A minor create a sense of expectancy, of increasing tension toward a nearing point of closure.

The repeated half note–quarter note rhythm that appears so prominently is often a Brahmsian metaphor for the loneliness resulting from separation. An aura of melancholy results from its combination with numerous neighboring tones.

Noteworthy features are the turn to the relative major for the cadence of the first section and the stretching to ten measures of the first phrase of the second section.

6.

Hungarian

Ein kleiner, hübscher Vogel nahm den Flug	A little, pretty bird took its flight into the
Zum Garten hin, da gab es Obst genug.	garden, where there was plenty of fruit.
Wenn ich ein hübscher, kleiner Vogel wär',	If I were a pretty little bird,
Ich säumte nicht, ich täte so wie der.	I wouldn't hesitate, I'd do the same as he.
Leimruten-Arglist lauert an dem Ort;	A snare of lime twigs lay in wait there;
Der arme Vogel konnte nicht mehr fort.	the poor bird could not escape.
Wenn ich ein hübscher, kleiner Vogel wär',	If I were a pretty little bird,
Ich säumte doch, ich täte nicht wie der.	I'd surely hesitate, I wouldn't do the same as he.
Der Vogel kam in eine schöne Hand,	The bird came into kindly hands,
Da tat es ihm, dem Glücklichen, nicht and.	which he didn't mind at all, the fortunate bird.
Wenn ich ein hübscher, kleiner Vogel wär',	If I were a pretty little bird,
Ich säumte nicht, ich täte doch wie der.	I wouldn't hesitate, I'd surely do the same as he.

A major; *Grazioso;* SATB.

Approximate duration: 2′35.

Rondo, A B B′ A′ codetta C A codetta; the C episode is itself a binary form.

The expected sense of structural significance arrives with this large-scale movement in A major. Its pairing with no. 5 recalls the analogous minor-major progression of nos. 2 and 3. The move to the key of the mediant for the B section evokes the early cadence on the mediant of no. 1, while the F major of the C episode echoes the key of no. 4. The finality of the closing punctuation makes it clear that the first large group of movements has come to an end.

The delicious Viennese lilt of the principal theme effectively suggests the soaring flight of the carefree bird. By contrast, the threat of the treacherous lime twigs is portrayed in short, anxious phrases and a frenzy of bustling staccato eighth notes. The kindly hands of stanza 3 elicit gentle music in the foreign key of the lowered submediant.

The movement features a particularly effective variety of color in the vocal scoring. Examples are the solo tenor beginning, his cadence gracefully eliding the entrance of the other three voices; the gradual addition of voices in the B episode; the contrast in the ensuing transition between the harmonized men's voices and the soprano in unison with the piano; and the changing timbre of the repeated motive in the concluding codetta.

7.

Polish

Wohl schön bewandt	Matters once stood
War es vorehe	quite nicely
Mit meinem Leben,	with my life,
Mit meiner Liebe;	with my love;
Durch eine Wand,	through a wall,
Ja, durch zehn Wände	indeed, through ten walls,
Erkannte mich	my boyfriend's eyes
Des Freundes Sehe:	recognized me:
Doch jetzo, wehe,	but now, alas,
Wenn ich dem Kalten	even if I stand
Auch noch so dicht	right in front
Vor'm Auge stehe,	of the cold one,
Es merkt's sein Auge,	his eyes notice me,
Sein Herze nicht.	but his heart doesn't.

C minor; S (A).

Approximate duration: 1′10.
Binary.
The initial unaccompanied A♭ is heard momentarily as the enharmonic

G♯, becoming in effect a single-note modulation. The temporary move to A major at the beginning of the second part helps to relate C minor to what has gone before.

A move to the lowered-submediant major in the first section is a metaphor for the happiness of the past; the return to C minor at the end represents the sadness of present reality, made even more poignant by passage through Neapolitan harmony en route. Lamenting second-beat dissonances at beginning and end suggest weeping.

There is some manuscript evidence that Brahms tried to remove the parallel fifths in the first two measures of the second part, but he apparently found no "correct" version that pleased him.

In piano *primo*, m. 4 of the second half, the Breitkopf & Härtel edition prints a ♯ for the lower note of the turn; it is lacking in the Peters edition.

8.

Polish

Wenn so lind dein Auge mir	When your eyes look at me
Und so lieblich schauet—	so gently and so lovingly,
Jede letzte Trübe fliehet,	every last care that
Welche mich umgrauet.	troubles me vanishes.
Dieser Liebe schöne Glut,	Don't let the lovely glow
Laß sie nicht verstieben!	of this love dissipate!
Nimmer wird, wie ich, so treu	Never will anyone else love you
Dich ein andrer lieben.	so truly as I.

A♭ major; SATB.

Approximate duration: 1′30.
Binary.

The quiet joy of requited love is characterized in caressing long appoggiaturas, leisurely hemiola at the cadences, and the gentle settling into major keys a third lower. A temporary move to E major in the second part forms a connection with the earlier sharp keys, and a further move to C major recalls the sequential constructions in nos. 2 and 3.

At "dich," five measures before the end, the downbeat G for the soprano lacks its ♭ in the Peters edition.

9.
Hungarian

Am Donaustrande, da steht ein Haus,
Da schaut ein rosiges Mädchen aus.
Das Mädchen, es ist wohl gut gehegt,
Zehn eiserne Riegel sind vor die Türe gelegt.

Zehn eiserne Riegel—das ist ein Spaß;
Die spreng' ich, als wären sie nur von Glas.

On the bank of the Danube, there stands a house,
where a rosy maiden looks out.
The maiden is very well guarded;
ten iron bars protect the door.

Ten iron bars—that is a joke!
I'll break them down as though they were only glass.

E major; SATB.

Approximate duration: 2'10.
Rounded binary.

The tonal descent of another (enharmonic) third arrives at the key of the cycle's beginning to conclude its first half.

The text begins with a quiet nature picture in which the Danube is prominent, proceeds to an image of the girl kept prisoner, and ends by expressing the bravado of the would-be liberator-suitor. Significantly, Brahms chooses also to recall the first couplet, ending this structural pillar with the image of the house by the Danube. One is reminded of Eduard Hanslick's comment when acknowledging Brahms's dedication to him of the Op. 39 waltzes for piano duet:

> Brahms and waltzes! The two words stare at each other in positive amazement on the elegant title page. The earnest, silent Brahms, a true younger brother of Schumann, and just as North German, Protestant, and unworldly as he—writing waltzes! There is only one word that solves the enigma, and that is—Vienna. (Kalbeck, Johannes Brahms, II$_1$, 193–94; Eng. trans. in Nieman, *Brahms*, trans. Phillips, 381)

Indeed many have found in "Am Donaustrande" a resemblance and homage to Johann Strauss's immensely popular "Blue Danube" waltz, first performed in Vienna on 13 February 1867.

Appropriately, the soprano, representing the constrained maiden, is silent during the discussion of her plight, joining in with the others only for the last couplet, which considers her release. The bass begins this segment with a variant of the opening motive. When the actual opening music returns at the end of the section, the tenor leads with a new countermelody which, joined by the bass, fills the rests between phrases of the melody.

The plagal cadence and fermata of the piano postlude contribute further to the concluding function of the movement.

10.

Russian-Polish Dance Song

O, wie sanft die Quelle sich	Oh, how gently the stream
Durch die Wiese windet;	meanders through the meadow!
O, wie schön, wenn Liebe sich	Oh, how lovely it is
Zu der Liebe findet!	when love is reciprocated!

G major; SATB.

Approximate duration: 0′55.
Binary.

This doorway to the second half of the set is distinguished by a fresh new key and phrases that are extended to ten measures by the appending of a two-measure hemiola figure. A rhythmic motive consisting of a dotted quarter and three eighth notes is pervasive.

In the first part the tenor imitates the soprano in free canon, and the added hemiola is for the piano alone. In the second part there are free canons between both the tenor and soprano and the alto and bass. The latter pair share the hemiola with the piano the first time, eliding the cadence; in the written-out repetition, the voices eschew the first hemiola but share in the second, which is appended both to accommodate the repetition of the last line of text and to confirm the tonic key for the final cadence.

The "gentleness" of the text is suggested by the lack of rhythmic complexity, a preference for subdominant harmony, and the broadening at the cadences. The male-female canons in the second half and the coming together of the voices at the end symbolize the happy discovery that love is mutual.

11.

Polish

Nein, es ist nicht auszukommen	No, there is no getting along
Mit den Leuten;	with people;
Alles wissen sie so giftig	they know how to interpret everything
Auszudeuten.	so maliciously.
Bin ich heiter, hegen soll ich	If I am cheerful, I must be harboring
Lose Triebe;	wicked desires;
Bin ich still, so heißt's, ich wäre	if I am quiet, they say I must
Irr, aus Liebe.	be lovelorn.

C minor; SATB.

Approximate duration: 0′52.

Rounded binary.

Despite their extreme dynamic difference, no. 11 proceeds smoothly from no. 10, beginning with its primary rhythmic motive and a repetition of its concluding harmony.

The mood, however, is no longer blissfully serene but agitated and irritable. Rhythms are diverse and active. Much of the accompaniment is staccato; *secondo* has nearly constant afterbeats in the principal section and gradually increasing rhythmic activity in the contrasting ten measures. Harmonies are limited almost entirely to tonic and dominant in the tonic key and its relative major, the gentler subdominant being avoided completely. The voice parts, though homophonic, are fast-moving and wordy; even the slight broadening at the end sounds more belligerent rather than conciliatory.

12.

Russian-Polish Dance Song

Schlosser auf! und mache Schlösser,	Up, locksmith, and make padlocks,
Schlösser ohne Zahl!	padlocks without number!
Denn die bösen Mäuler will ich	Because I want to seal up the malicious
Schließen allzumal.	tongues, every one of them.

E♭ major; SATB.

Approximate duration: 0'45.
Binary.
With hardly a pause for breath, a repetition of the bass G-G-C from the last measure of no. 11, now metrically displaced, propels the tirade forward. The initial harmony repeats the concluding one of no. 11, and the first full measure for all four voices recalls the dotted quarter–three eighths rhythmic motive.

But overall the mood is now more decisive than testy, aided by the poem's strong final syllables. C-minor and E♭-major harmonies again alternate, but this time E♭ major prevails. Quarter notes predominate in the voice parts and, except for the onomatopoeic repetition of "denn die bösen Mäuler," there are fewer successive eighth notes than before.

To initiate each segment, the bass repeats the motive with which he began the piece. The tenor joins him in moving independently of the other voices at the end of each half, producing a texture that is lightly contrapuntal though mostly homophonic.

13.
Russian-Polish Dance Song

Vögelein durchrauscht die Luft,	The little bird darts through the air,
Sucht nach einem Aste;	searching for a branch;
Und das Herz, ein Herz begehrt's,	and the heart yearns for another heart,
Wo es selig raste.	where it may blissfully come to rest.

A♭ major; SA.

Approximate duration: 0'45.
Binary.
Graceful serenity comes as a welcome relief to the preceding acrimony. The key relates to that of no. 12 as tonic to dominant.

Piano *primo*'s two-note slurs in the first part represent the darting bird; in the second part, yearning harmonies and a flowing eighth-note figure that appears in *primo* and *secondo* in alternate phrases suggest the seeking of one heart for another.

The most striking feature of the movement is the interplay between hemiola and normal triple meter. Of the four four-measure phrases, hemiola appears in the first (in the voices and piano *secondo*) and fourth (piano *primo* only); in that regard, the second half thus mirrors the first.

14.
Russian-Polish Dance Song

Sieh, wie ist die Welle klar,	See how clear the waves are,
Blickt der Mond hernieder!	as the moon looks down!
Die du meine Liebe bist,	You who are my sweetheart,
Liebe du mich wieder.	return my love!

E♭ major; TB.

Approximate duration: 0′50.

In the third line of the text, Brahms changed the original "Liebste" to "Liebe."

A duet for male voices is evidently intended as a counterpart to the preceding duet for female voices. The structure of two eight-measure periods is the same, the quiet mood prevails, and the keys relate as tonic and dominant. The accompaniment of the opening phrase even has reminiscences of the flowing eighth-note figure and hemiola with which no. 13 ended.

The recalling in the second part of the dotted quarter–three eighths rhythmic motive that figured so prominently in no. 10 may be a deliberate reference to the requited love with which that movement concerned itself. The turn to the lowered submediant in m. 5 tints the moon's glance with enchantment. At that point in his own copy of the first edition, Brahms replaced the "*p*" in the voice parts with "*dolce*" and added a "*pp*" in the piano parts.

15.
Russian-Polish Dance Song

Nachtigall, sie singt so schön,	The nightingale, it sings so sweetly
Wenn die Sterne funkeln,—	when the stars twinkle;
Liebe mich, geliebtes Herz,	love me, dear heart,
Küsse mich im Dunkeln!	kiss me in the darkness!

A♭ major; SATB.

Approximate duration: 1′20.
Binary.
Rhythmically linked to no. 14 and growing out of its tonic pitch, the movement features a prominent dotted-rhythm countermelody in piano *primo*. In the first half the *secondo* doubles the voices; in the second, it recalls the melody of the first half while the voices present spacious new independent melodic material.

Static harmonies and a bass pedal point in the piano create an aura of tender calm in the opening phrase. The pulsations on E♭ in piano *primo* suggest the singing of the nightingale; as the figure ascends into the upper register, it seems also to portray the twinkling stars.

An enharmonic shift into the key of the lowered mediant lends ardor to "liebe mich, geliebtes Herz." A gradual chromatic return to the tonic combines with hemiola in the accompaniment to suffuse "küsse mich" with wonder. The two-measure repetition of "im Dunkeln" of the first ending is extended to five measures as postlude, the voices sharing in the piano's series of harmonies. The plagal cadence and borrowed F♭ add a final caress.

16.

Hungarian

Ein dunkeler Schacht ist Liebe,	Love is a dark shaft,
Ein gar zu gefährlicher Bronnen;	a far too dangerous well;
Da fiel ich hinein, ich Armer,	I fell right into it, poor me,
Kann weder hören, noch seh'n.	and can neither hear nor see;
Nur denken an meine Wonnen,	I can only think of my joy,
Nur stöhnen in meinen Weh'n.	only moan in my pain.

F minor; *Lebhaft* (lively); SATB.

Approximate duration: 1′20.
Binary.
Unrest results from the constant eighth notes (often broken octaves) in the accompaniment and the lightly contrapuntal texture. The bass en-

trance in m. 2 inverts the initial motive of the other voices; in mm. 8–9 and 12–13 the bass has the original motive, which the soprano inverts in mm. 10–11 and 14–15. The successive entrances of "nur denken an meine Wonnen" alternate the inversion with the original shape.

Some amusing instances of word painting are the drop of an octave in the bass part between "Ein dunkeler Schacht" and "ist Liebe"; the plunge into the low register of piano *secondo* in m. 10, after "da fiel ich hinein"; and the near silence that follows "kann weder hören, noch seh'n" in mm. 14–17.

"Nur denken an meine Wonnen" in mm. 18–26 elicits a turn to the major mode and long contemplative blocks of dominant-seventh harmony on C and F. The repetitions of "stöhnen" are harmonized with a painful diminished seventh, which resolves to F major in m. 28 and F minor in m. 30; finally the addition of a bass C at "meinen" in m. 33 transforms it into an even more painful dominant ninth to initiate the cadence.

The second ending derives vehemence from its *sforzando,* a *crescendo* to *forte,* and the higher register of its final chord.

17.
Hungarian

Nicht wandle, mein Licht, dort außen	Don't wander, light of my life, outside there
Im Flurbereich!	in the meadowland!
Die Füße würden dir, die zarten,	Your dainty feet would get
Zu naß, zu weich.	too wet, too tender.
All überströmt sind dort die Wege,	There the routes, the footpaths you would
Die Stege dir;	take, are all flooded;
So überreichlich tränte dorten	there such a torrent of tears over-flowed
Das Auge mir.	from my eyes.

D♭ major; *Mit Ausdruck* (with expression); T.

Approximate duration: 1′55.
Binary.
Frequent downbeat rests and breathless, short fragments of melody lend an air of caring concern to the vocal line. The use of F♭ throughout

phrase 3 (mm. 11–15) and its stretching to five measures enhance its evocation of tenderness. The similar stretching of "so überreichlich tränte dorten" in the second part combines with appoggiaturas, a digression to the key of the subdominant, and chromaticism borrowed from the minor to make the phrase poignant.

The scalar quarter notes that appear in piano *secondo* at the end of the first section underlie the whole of the first phrase of the second section, perhaps suggesting the widespread flooding that the text describes; piano *primo* makes use of the same motive at the climaxes of both stretched phrases, ascending in the first part and descending in the second.

18.

Hungarian

Es bebet das Gesträuche;	The shrubbery is quivering;
Gestreift hat es im Fluge	a little bird in flight
Ein Vöglein.	has brushed against it.
In gleicher Art erbebet,	That's the way my soul
Die Seele mir erschüttert	trembles, unsettled
Von Liebe, Lust und Leide,	by love, joy, and anguish
Gedenkt sie dein.	when I think of you.

D♭/C♯ major; *Lebhaft* (lively); SATB.

Approximate duration: 1′25.
Rounded binary.
The movement consists entirely of four-measure phrases, to which the piano adds two measures each of introduction and postlude. The first section has a pair of phrases in B♭ minor (the relative minor) and another pair in D♭ major (the tonic). The second section has the key signature of C♯ minor, but its first two phrases begin in E (the relative major), the first moving to A minor and the second to B minor. There ensue two phrases that modulate to C♯ minor; the first arrives at the dominant and the second at the subdominant, where a chromatic alteration shifts the mode to major. The remaining two phrases are virtually identical to those that ended the first part, but they are notated in the enharmonically equivalent C♯ major.

Why this peculiar succession of relatives, enharmonics, and changes of key signature? One can only conjecture that the beginning in B♭ minor is to freshen the sound of D♭ major, which is the key of the preceding movement. It seems likely too that the key-signature change to four sharps is intended to relate the end of the work visually to its beginning, particularly since the first phrase in the new section touches E major and A minor, the keys of the first two movements. There can be little doubt that the like section endings are notated enharmonically in order to underscore Daumer's analogy between the little bird, who sets the shrubbery aquiver, and the lover, the thought of whom causes the same reaction in the poet's soul, while allowing each to retain its own identity.

In the opening phrases the barely moving vocal lines in *pianissimo* staccato quarter notes combine with the shimmering piano treble to portray the quavering bushes. By contrast, a soaring melodic line suggests the flight of the bird. In the second part, the parallel construction but rising pitch of the first two phrase pairs evokes the growing agitation of the poet. The rests inserted into "von Liebe, Lust und Leide" illustrate his unease, and the dissonant harmonizations of "Leide" are similarly metaphoric.

The movement serves admirably as a conclusion to the set. Like the others that Brahms placed in ending positions (nos. 6 and 9), its relatively enlarged form lends it weight among its simple binary neighbors. In combination with no. 17, it also acquires gravity from the prolongation of D♭ as a tonal center. The generally low dynamic level, the broadened note values of the closing phrases, and the final *diminuendo* combine to create a quality of epilogue. Just as the change to sharp keys recalls the beginning of the cycle, the piano *primo*'s closing appoggiaturas sound as distant reminders of those that figured so prominently in the first movement.

Four Duets for Soprano and Alto

OPUS 61

Duette für Sopran und Alt mit Begleitung des Pianoforte von Johannes Brahms (Duets for soprano and alto with piano accompaniment by Johannes Brahms), Op. 61. Published, together with the second edition of the Op. 20 duets, in September 1874 by N. Simrock in Berlin; publication number 7452; texts in both German and English.

Since the texts of these duets do not suggest two independent voices (the sisters of no. 1 are so alike that they sing as one), Brahms sets aside the dramatic dialogue style of Op. 28 and reverts to the *Hausmusik* style of Op. 20. Here, as there, the second voice is used primarily to add sonorous richness, secondarily for the textual emphasis and textural contrast of occasional counterpoint.

The four duets are gratifying to perform, either singly or as a group; each is a distinct, highly refined entity, and the four contrast agreeably.

Die Schwestern, Op. 61/1 (The sisters)
Text by Eduard Mörike (1804–1875)

Wir Schwestern zwei, wir schönen,
So gleich von Angesicht,
So gleich kein Ei dem andern,
Kein Stern dem andern nicht.

Wir Schwestern zwei, wir schönen,
Wir haben nußbraun' Haar,

We two sisters, we pretty ones,
we look so alike,
no egg is so identical to another,
nor any star to another.

We two sisters, we pretty ones,
we have nut-brown hair,

Und flichtst du sie in einen Zopf,
Man kennt sie nicht fürwahr.

Wir Schwestern zwei, wir schönen,
Wir tragen gleich Gewand,
Spazieren auf dem Wiesenplan
Und singen Hand in Hand.

Wir Schwestern zwei, wir schönen,
Wir spinnen in die Wett',
Wir sitzen an einer Kunkel,
Wir schlafen in einem Bett.

O Schwestern zwei, ihr schönen!
Wie hat sich das Blättchen gewand't!
Ihr liebet einerlei Liebchen—
(Und) jetzt hat das Liedel ein End'.

and if you wove it into one pigtail,
you couldn't tell which was which.

We two sisters, we pretty ones,
we wear matching dresses,
we stroll in the meadow
and sing, hand in hand.

We two sisters, we pretty ones,
we spin in rivalry,
we sit at one distaff,
we sleep in the same bed.

O sisters two, you pretty ones!
How the tide has turned!
You love the same sweetheart—
now the little song is over!

G minor/major; $\frac{2}{4}$; *Allegretto;* SA.

Approximate duration: 1'55.
Varied strophic.

The date of composition is not known, but the duet is included in Brahms's 1860 list of still unpublished songs and duets. George Bozarth speculates (in "Brahms's Duets," 196) that "Die Schwestern" may have originated in the autumn of 1858, which would make it contemporaneous not only with Brahms's first great involvement with folk materials (1856–1858) but also with "An eine Äolsharfe," Op. 19/4 (composed in September 1858) and, very possibly, an early version of "Agnes," Op. 59/5, his other two settings of Mörike texts. Handwriting characteristics in the extant sources indicate that "Die Schwestern" was thoroughly revised in the early 1870s, converted probably from simple strophic to its final varied strophic form through the reworking of its closing strophe.

Recha Büchler and Marie Pfliger sang the first public performance on 24 April 1880 in Vienna. A private performance had taken place on 29 January 1878 at Billroth's house.

The text is from Mörike's *Gedichte* (Stuttgart and Tübingen, 1838). The original has "gewend't" instead of "gewand't" in verse 5 and "lichtbraune Haar" instead of "nußbraun' Haar" in verse 2. Bolstering Bozarth's defense of a composition date of 1858 is the possibility that Brahms's darkening of the sisters' hair was in homage to the brunette Agathe von Siebold (see the general notes for Op. 20) and her friend Bertha Wagner, who were the recipients of the two Op. 20 "Weg der Liebe" duets in September 1858.

Like Mörike's poem, Brahms's setting is a sophisticated evocation of folklore, but with an ironic jolt near the end. The principal strophe comprises two kindred phrases, each with an initial rising arpeggio and an interior repetition, and a closing ritornello for the piano. The first phrase, of six measures, opens in the tonic G minor, has a one-measure repetition ("wir schönen"), and modulates to the dominant. The second has a beginning arpeggio on the minor dominant, its interior repetition is of two measures ("kein Ei dem andern"), and it is extended to eight measures by the repetition also of its two-measure tonic cadence pattern.

The sisters sing four stanzas to the same nuanceless music (though strophes 3 and 4 have a different accompaniment that features arpeggios downward)—two about how alike they look and two about how similarly they behave. Their twinship is demonstrated in their simultaneous declamation of text and their unison singing to begin and end each strophe.

But strophe 5 opens *forte* in G major, and a new double persona, presumably a narrator (though Raphael Atlas makes a case for the flesh-and-blood reality of the sisters themselves, hidden until now by their doll-like exteriors ["Text and Musical Gesture," 242]), addresses them as "*ihr* schönen" (*you* pretty ones), and lays bare the disturbing admission that both are in love with the same man. Adding emphasis, each half of the closing couplet is lengthened to six measures by text repetition. In the first half ("Ihr liebet einerlei Liebchen"), the arpeggios, both rising and falling, move into the accompaniment, while the voices leapfrog over each other four times, producing clashing dissonances as they rise (mm. 79–83). In the second half ("jetzt hat das Liedel ein End'") the text is interrupted by rests, and there is a gradual quieting of the rhythmic motion, as though the singers were reluctant to let the song come to an end. Perhaps there is more that the narrator-persona could reveal, or perhaps the sisters only gradually face the realization that their once-perfect duality can no longer exist.

The piano ritornello begins in the tonic major but soon reverts to the original minor, now strangely sadder than before.

Klosterfräulein, Op. 61/2 (The young nun)

Text by Justinus Kerner (1786–1862)

Ach, ach, ich armes Klosterfräulein!
O Mutter, was hast du gemacht!
Lenz ging am Gitter vorüber
Und hat mir kein Blümlein gebracht!

Ach, ach, wie weit hier unten
Zwei Schäflein gehen im Tal.
Viel Glück, ihr Schäflein, ihr sahet
Den Frühling zum ersten Mal.

Alas, alas, wretched nun that I am!
Oh, Mother, what you have wrought!
Spring passed by the lattice
and brought no little flower to me!

Alas, alas, so far below
two lambs are roaming in the valley.
How lucky, you lambkins, you saw
spring for the first time.

Ach, ach, wie weit hier oben
Zwei Vöglein fliegen in Ruh!
Viel Glück, ihr Vöglein, ihr flieget
Der besseren Heimat zu.

Alas, alas, so far above
two little birds are flying in peace.
how lucky, you fledglings, you fly
toward a better place.

A minor; $\frac{2}{4}$; *Andante;* SA.

Approximate duration: 1′55.
Strophic.
Composed in September 1852, the earliest extant duet.
    The first performance was given at a Brahms festival in Merseburg on 21 February 1895 by Marie Berg and Amalie Joachim with Brahms at the piano.
    Kerner's poem was printed in Leo von Seckendorff's *Musenalmanach* for 1807. It was also included in the Kretzschmer-Zuccalmaglio *Deutsche Volkslieder mit ihren Original-Weisen* (Berlin, 1838–1840) under the title "Altes Volkslied" (Old folk song). (In the 1852 autograph in the Library of Congress, Brahms's duet setting is entitled "Lied im Volkston" [Song in folk style].)
    Three-measure phrases are the rule, reflecting the poem's triple meter. The introspective repetition in augmentation at the end occupies four measures to round off the strophe satisfyingly.
    The declamation of text is synchronous throughout with the sole exception of m. 5. Since it is clear from the opening line that the poet has used the first person singular, the addition of a second voice seems curious, but its sound evokes the thought that the young nun of the title may speak for generations of other unhappy novices.
    The sound of the music, with its Phrygian cadences and its G♯/G♮ ambivalence, is archaic, and the floating tenth-to-octave closing cadence communicates timelessness.
    The piano contributes to the first strophe's lack of stability through its prolonged unresolved bass E and its mournful little sighs inserted between phrases. The sounding of the A as bass at the beginning of strophe 2 shows in an instant that focus has shifted to the exterior world. Strophe 3 is marked as climactic by its *forte* and its more active accompaniment. The right hand's triplets suggest both the activity of flying and (in mm. 38–39) the disappearance of the birds into the distance. As the dynamic level of the remainder of the strophe decreases progressively, hope seems to decline, and the harmonization of the final octave E with A minor rather than the anticipated E major conveys a profound sense of weary resignation.

Phänomen, Op. 61/3 (Phenomenon)

Text by Johann Wolfgang von Goethe (1749–1832)

Wenn zu der Regenwand
Phöbus sich gattet,
Gleich steht ein Bogenrand
Farbig beschattet.

Im Nebel gleichen Kreis
Seh' ich gezogen,
Zwar ist der Bogen weiß,
Doch Himmelsbogen.

So sollst du, munt'rer Greis,
Dich nicht betrüben;
Sind gleich die Haare weiß,
Doch wirst du lieben.

When Phoebus weds himself
to the bank of rainclouds,
an arch is outlined,
shaded with color.

In the mist I see described
a similar circle;
admittedly the arc is white,
but a rainbow all the same.

So you should not be
downcast, lively old man;
although your hair is white,
yet you will love.

B major; $\frac{3}{4}$; *Poco Andante;* SA.

Approximate duration: 2'05.
Varied strophic; A B A.
Composed December 1873/January 1874.
The first performance was sung (together with "Die Boten der Liebe," Op. 61/4) on 5 February 1884 in Basel by Ida Huber-Petzold and Agnes Scholer.
The text is from Goethe's *West-Östlicher Diwan, Buch des Sängers* (1814). Phoebus was the Roman sun god.
November and December of 1873 saw the publication of Brahms's Haydn Variations, Op. 56, and the two Op. 51 string quartets. The contrapuntal mastery which they exhibit was not limited to those works, however, and several songs from that period (this one among them) are filled with contrapuntal devices. See, for example, "Mein wundes Herz," Op. 59/7, composed during spring 1873, or "An ein Bild," Op. 63/3, composed during the following summer.
One of the glories of Brahmsian counterpoint is that it flows so naturally that, except in such obvious situations as canon between principal voices, the listener is barely aware of it. (On 27 April 1856, during their mutual study of counterpoint, Brahms wrote to Joachim regarding some canons enclosed therewith: "The craft aside, is it good music? Does the artifice make it more beautiful and valuable?") Even one who has heard

"Phänomen" many times might not be aware that the motive formed by the last four melody notes of the introduction—B-A♯-C♯-F♯—recurs alternately in the soprano voice and piano bass every two measures in the principal strophe, excepting only the cadence. (The last note of the bass transposition in m. 11 may be found in the half-note chord of m. 12 or as the downbeat octave of m. 13.)

The canonic imitation that begins the second strophe ("Im Nebel gleichen Kreis") uses an inversion of the same motive, and both entrances are supported by the original motive in the bass. The other canonic melody ("Zwar ist der Bogen weiß") outlines the same intervals in reverse order—fifth, third, second. The repeated "doch Himmelsbogen" that ends the strophe is set to two statements of the original motive at the original pitch, preparing the way for the return of the music of strophe 1, its accompaniment somewhat enriched sonorously, for stanza 3.

The expressive postlude concludes the piece with a final appearance of the motive in satisfying augmentation.

Curiously, the effect of this economical use of materials is not cerebration but spontaneity, as though the piece had sprung from a single flash of inspiration. Particularly noteworthy is the interrelatedness of the voices and piano.

Concerning "Phänomen," the noted Munich opera conductor and Brahms advocate Hermann Levi wrote to Brahms on 24 December 1874:

> The B-major melody "Wenn zu der Regenwand" is so constantly with me that in a last effort to rid myself of it I must take paper and write to you. If only I could tell you how much the song has impressed and moved me! (*Briefwechsel*, VII, 178; Eng. trans. in Friedländer, *Brahms's Lieder*, trans. Leese, 106–107)

Die Boten der Liebe, Op. 61/4 (Love's messengers)

Translated from the Bohemian by Joseph Wenzig (1807–1876)

Wie viel schon der Boten	Yea, how many messengers
Flogen die Pfade	rushed down the paths
Vom Walde herunter,	from the woods,
Boten der Treu';	messengers of faithfulness;
Trugen mir Briefchen	brought me tidings
Dort aus der Ferne,	from a great distance,
Trugen mir Briefchen	brought tidings to me
Vom Liebsten herbei!	here from my beloved!
Wie viel schon der Lüfte	Yea, how many breezes
Wehten vom Morgen,	have blown since morning,
Wehten bis Abends	blown until evening
So schnell ohne Ruh',	so briskly without respite;

Trugen mir Küßchen	brought me kisses
Vom kühligen Wasser,	over the cooling water,
Trugen mir Küßchen	brought kisses to me
Vom Liebsten herzu!	here from my beloved!
Wie wiegten die Halme	How the growing crops swayed
Auf grünenden Bergen,	on the verdant hills,
Wie wiegten die Ähren	how the heads of grain swayed
Auf Feldern sich leis',	gently in the fields;
Mein goldenes Liebchen,	"My golden sweetheart,"
Lispelten alle,	they all whispered,
Mein goldenes Liebchen,	"my golden sweetheart,
Ich lieb' dich so heiß.	I love you so ardently."

D major; $\frac{9}{8}$; *Vivace;* SA.

Approximate duration: 2′45.
Strophic.
Composed December 1873/January 1874.

The first performance was given in Zurich on 19 December 1876 by Frau Suter-Weber and Frau Hegar-Volkart.

The text is from Wenzig's *Westslawischer Märchenschatz* (Leipzig, 1857), which Brahms owned.

The ardor of the setting derives from almost every element of its construction; among them are its fast tempo and the breathless skipping of the accompaniment. The second full measure introduces two important motives under slurs—a fervent rising quarter-eighth figure and a tender stepwise descent, dotted quarter to quarter.

The strophe proper comprises three sections, each rising to a higher pitch and using longer durations. The first emphasizes and moves to the dominant, and the melody rises twice to F♯; repetition of the fourth line of text lengthens the section to ten measures. The second section, also extended to ten measures by an interior repetition of line 7, stresses the subdominant, and its melodic rise to G is supported by rising sequence and a crescendo to *forte;* dotted half notes appear for the first time. Repetitions of the last couplet make up the text of section 3, whose opening sequences rise to a climactic final phrase stressing the supertonic, altered to become the dominant's dominant as the cadence nears. The crux of the entire strophe is the soprano's rise *forte* to the high A as her final "Liebsten" ("lieb' dich" in strophe 3) is elongated to span seven beats, overlapping the start of a two-measure cadential hemiola that affects the second- and third-to-last syllables of text. Rather than structural text repetition, it is this characteristic Brahmsian broadening to the cadence that expands the third section also to ten measures. The alto's repetition of three syllables both emphasizes the key words and anchors the meter during the soprano's hemiola.

Except for minor discrepancies in the use of upbeats, musically the three strophes are virtually identical. The postlude counters the introduction's upward leaps by plunging to a sonorous conclusion in the piano's lower middle register.

Three Quartets

OPUS 64

Quartette für vier Solostimmen mit Pianoforte von Johannes Brahms (Quartets for four solo voices with piano by Johannes Brahms), Op. 64. Published in November 1874 by C. F. Peters of Leipzig and Berlin; publication numbers 5705 (score) and 5706 (parts); German only.

The three quartets are substantial and imaginative, true vocal chamber music. There is nothing in the first two texts to suggest multiple voices, but Brahms sets them in his characteristic sonorous Lied *cum* string quartet style. Similar treatment combines the soprano, alto, and bass into the "Ich" of the dialogue "Fragen," the role of the lovesick heart being assigned to the solo tenor.

In a letter dated the month before their publication, Brahms remarked to the publisher that the Op. 64 quartets "might on occasion be sung by a small choir." It is not clear whether this concession was an acknowledgment of the size and weight of the quartets or of the shrinking market for domestic music of such difficulty.

An die Heimat, Op. 64/1 (To my homeland)
Text by C. O. Sternau (pseudonym of Otto Inkermann)

Heimat!	Homeland!
Wunderbar tönendes Wort!	Wondrously resounding word!
Wie auf befiederten Schwingen	As though on feathered wings
Ziehst du mein Herz zu dir fort.	you draw my heart to you.

Jubelnd, als müßt ich den Gruß	Rejoicing, as if I were to bring you
Jeglicher Seele dir bringen,	the greeting of every kindred spirit,
Trag' ich zu dir meinen Fuß,	I direct my feet to you,
Freundliche Heimat!	benevolent homeland!

Heimat!	Homeland!
Bei dem sanft klingenden Ton	At that softly ringing sound
Wecken mich alte Gesänge,	I am roused by old songs,
Die in der Ferne mich flohn;	which in the distance escaped me;
Rufen mir freudenvoll zu	the enticing pealing of bells calls
Heimatlich lockende Klänge:	me homeward, filled with joy.
Du nur allein bist die Ruh',	You alone are my repose,
Schützende Heimat!	sheltering homeland!

Heimat!	Homeland!
Gib mir den Frieden zurück,	Restore to me the peace
Den ich im Weiten verloren,	that I lost far away,
Gib mir dein blühendes Glück!	grant me your thriving good fortune!
Unter den Bäumen am Bach,	Under the trees by the brook,
Wo ich vor Zeiten geboren,	where I was born long ago,
Gib mir ein schützendes Dach,	provide me a protecting roof,
Liebende Heimat!	loving homeland!

G major; $\frac{3}{4}$; *Bewegt, doch nicht zu schnell* (agitatedly, but not too fast); SATB.

Approximate duration: 4'50.

Through-composed, with elements of strophic variation; three dissimilar sections that end alike, plus coda.

Composed summer 1864 in Vienna.

The original version was performed in Vienna on 7 April 1867 by Anna Schmidtler, Nelly Lumpe, Gustav Krenn, and Herr Malferteiner, with Brahms at the piano. The published form had its first Vienna hearing (together with "Der Abend," Op. 64/2) on 24 February 1875, sung by Adele Passy-Cornet, Fräulein Tomsa, Herr von der Tann, and Herr Buchholz.

The text is from Sternau's *Gedichte* (Berlin, 1851).

The deeply felt setting is among the most richly detailed and complex pieces of Brahms's vocal chamber music. There seems little doubt that its emotional intensity results from the displaced North German's empathy with the poet's nostalgia for the land of his birth.

Unity is provided by the half note–quarter note rhythm and *crescendo-diminuendo*, same-harmony settings of the isolated word "Heimat!" with which each stanza begins; the achingly beautiful imitative music to which the closing line of every stanza is set; and the gently undulating double-note arpeggios that accompany both.

The music for the body of stanza 1 is freely canonic, suggesting the pull and persistence of thoughts of home. The identical rhythm and similar shape of the two statements of "wunderbar tönendes Wort!" set the stage. All four voices enter into one canon at "Wie auf befiederten Schwingen" and another at "Jubelnd, als müßt ich den Gruß," the latter having six entries before working its way toward the half-cadence in E♭ in mm. 28–29. The repeated-chord triplet accompaniment adds agitation; the unstable tonality effectively evokes yearning. Gradually the activity lessens, and "trag' ich zu dir meinen Fuß" is set in longer note values to music that is contrapuntal but no longer canonic. The inexorable slow return to the tonic G major is a metaphor for this line of text.

The second large section, by contrast, is almost entirely homophonic, often with contrary motion between the outer voices. An affecting turn to C minor marks the "alte Gesänge"; another to B major, the "heimatlich lockende Klänge." At "du nur allein bist die Ruh'," the double-note arpeggios reappear in the piano, and almost imperceptibly the tenor begins the imitative closing music, overlapping the cadence.

A change to the tonic minor, a new accompaniment figure in twining triplets (evoking the "brook" of the text), and the return of contrapuntal, even fugal, texture announce the third stanza. The tenor's initial subject is taken up by the alto and, later, the soprano at "Unter den Bäumen am Bach." At "gib mir ein schützendes Dach," the tonic major returns joyously with a supporting rise to *forte*. A broadening cadence in *diminuendo* prepares the tender closing music, to which is appended a coda, *più Adagio* and slowing, that revisits the "brook" accompanying figure amid numerous poignant chromaticisms and references to the minor. Accompanied by the customary double-note arpeggios and marked *più Lento,* a final, expanded, *crescendo-diminuendo* "Heimat!" brings the piece to a touching, tranquil close.

Der Abend, Op. 64/2 (Evening)

Text by Friedrich von Schiller (1759–1805)

Senke, strahlender Gott, die Fluren dürsten
Nach erquickendem Tau, der Mensch verschmachtet,
　Matter ziehen die Rosse,
　Senke den Wagen hinab.

Siehe, wer aus des Meers kristall'ner Woge

Sink, radiant god, the meadows thirst
for refreshing dew, man languishes,
　the horses pull more weakly—
　let the chariot sink downward.

Look who motions to you from the ocean's crystalline waves,

Lieblich lächelnd dir winkt! Erkennt
        dein Herz sie?
Rascher fliegen die Rosse,
    Tethys, die göttliche, winkt.

Schnell vom Wagen herab in ihre
        Arme
Springt der Führer, den Zaum ergreift
        Kupido,
    Stille halten die Rosse,
        Trinken die kühlende Flut.

An dem Himmel herauf mit leisen
        Schritten
Kommt die duftende Nacht; ihr folgt
        die süße
    Liebe. Ruhet und liebet!
        Phöbus, der liebende, ruht.

smiling lovingly! Does your heart
        recognize her?
The horses fly faster,
    the divine Tethys is beckoning.

Quickly the driver springs down from
        the chariot
into her arms, Cupid seizes the
        bridle,
    the horses keep quiet,
        drink the cooling water.

The fragrant night creeps up to the
        heavens
with soft steps; it is followed by
        sweet
    love. Rest ye and love!
        The amorous Phoebus is sleeping.

G minor/major; $\frac{3}{4}$; *Ruhig* (quietly); SATB.

Approximate duration: 4′30.
A B B′ A′.
Composed summer 1874 at Rüschlikon.

The first performance, together with that of "An die Heimat," Op. 64/1, took place on 24 February 1875 at a concert by the Singakademie in Vienna; the singers were Adele Passy-Cornet, Fräulein Tomsa, Herr von der Tann, and Herr Buchholz. (A review in the *Allgemeine deutsche Musikzeitung* for 5 March 1875 reports that two unspecified quartets from Op. 64 were sung in Leipzig on 14 February 1875; if one of the two was "Der Abend," that performance would have predated the Vienna performance by ten days. The singers in the Leipzig performance were Minna Reschka-Leutner, Fräulein Redeker, Herr Reinhold, and Herr Feßler.)

The text is from Schiller's *Gedichte,* Part 1, Book 1 (1800), where it appears with the title "Nach einem Gemälde" (After a painting). Brahms owned both an edition of the *Gedichte* (Leipzig, 1818) and the *Sämtliche Werke* (Stuttgart and Tübingen, 1847).

As the last line makes clear, the "radiant god" of line 1 is Phoebus, the customary Roman epithet for Apollo in his role as sun god. Tethys was a Titaness, the daughter of Uranus and Gaia; she married Oceanus, her brother, to whom she bore a multitude of offspring, including most of the river gods and their three thousand sisters, the Oceanids.

The setting contrasts two principal materials related by their rhythm and phrase structure. The first is restrained and dignified, befitting the evocation of figures from classical mythology; the second is warmer and more passionate, appropriate to the description of an amorous encounter.

Musical metaphors abound. The slow harmonic rhythm and lagging bass of stanza 1 suggest the pervading enervation it describes. The fatigue of the horses is portrayed in mm. 17–20 by the further broadening of what is already near absence of motion. The chariot's sinking is mirrored in the overall descent of all four voices and, less predictably, by the lower voices' imitation of the higher at the fifth below. The piano's slowly undulating arpeggios in stanza 2 depict the ocean's waves and, later, Tethys's appearance in m. 47; its triplets in *forte*, the quickened motion of the horses. In stanza 3, the sudden activity of the driver's descent into the goddess's arms and the transfer of the reins to Cupid is reflected in the agitation of descending triplets over ascending eighth notes. The hush as the horses are at last allowed to rest and satisfy their thirst is eloquently evoked by the soprano-tenor and alto-bass unisons in almost static canon against the deliberate descent of the bass to its goal of dominant. The ascent of night to the heavens in stanza 4 elicits a change to the tonic major and a broad arch of piano-treble melody, which dissolves into sighing appoggiatura chords as "sweet love follows." The same music that illustrated the horses' weakness in stanza 1 now accompanies the poet's behest to "rest and love"; the ensuing general descent, now extended from seven to eleven measures and continued by the postlude, portrays Phoebus's sleep.

Eusebius Mandyczewski believed that the parallel octaves that appear between the alto and bass voices beginning at the word "Liebe" in m. 89 (p. 41) of the Peters edition are incorrect; accordingly, his edition for Breitkopf & Härtel retains the alto G throughout mm. 89–91 (as in the analogous mm. 17–19), dropping to the E only at the second syllable of "liebet" in m. 92.

Fragen, Op. 64/3 (Questions)

Translated from the Turkish by Georg Friedrich Daumer (1800–1875)

(Ich sprach zum Herzen:)	(I said to my heart:)
"Mein liebes Herz, was ist dir?"	"My dear heart, what's the problem?"
(Es sprach:)	(It said:)
"Ich bin verliebt, das ist mir."	"I am in love, that's my problem."
(Ich sprach:)	(I said:)
"Wie ist dir denn zu Mut?"	"How do you feel then?"
(Es sprach:)	(It said:)
"Ich brenn' in Höllenglut."	"I am burning in hellfire."
(Ich sprach:)	(I said:)
"Erquicket dich kein Schlummer?"	"Does no sleep refresh you?"

(Es sprach:)
"Den litte Qual und Kummer?"
(Ich sprach:)
"Gelingt kein Widerstand?"
(Es sprach:)
"Wie doch bei solchem Band?"
(Ich sprach:)
"Ich hoffe, Zeit wird's wenden."
(Es sprach:)
"Es wird's der Tod nur enden."
(Ich sprach:)
"Was gäbst du, sie zu sehn?"
(Es sprach:)
"Mich, dich, Welt, Himmelshöhn."

(Ich sprach:)
"Du redest ohne Sinn."
(Es sprach:)
"Weil ich in Liebe bin."
(Ich sprach:)
"Du mußt vernünftig sein."
(Es sprach:)
"Das heißt, so kalt wie Stein."
(Ich sprach:)
"Du wirst zu Grunde gehen!"
(Es sprach:)
"Ach, möcht' es bald geschehen!"

(It said:)
"When afflicted by pain and grief?"
(I said:)
"No resistance succeeds?"
(It said:)
"How could it with such a bond?"
(I said:)
"I hope that time will change it."
(It said:)
"Only death will end it."
(I said:)
"What would you give to see her?"
(It said:)
"Myself, you, the earth, the heights
of heaven."
(I said:)
"You speak nonsense."
(It said:)
"Because I am in love."
(I said:)
"You must be reasonable."
(It said:)
"In other words, as cold as stone."
(I said:)
"You will perish!"
(It said:)
"Ah, the sooner the better!"

A major; $^6_8$; *Andante con moto;* SATB.

Approximate duration: 3′05.

Through-composed, with the effect of rondo (A B A′ C A″ coda).

The date of composition is uncertain. Brahms's register indicates that the quartet was composed in Vienna, though Kalbeck assigns it to Rüschlikon bei Zürich (*Johannes Brahms,* III₁, 34).

The first performance took place on 13 February 1875 in Mannheim, with Ottilie Ottiker, Frau Seubert-Hauser, Herr Jäger, and Herr Starke.

The text appears in *Polydora, ein weltpoetisches Liederbuch* (Frankfurt am Main, 1855). The reason for Brahms's change of Daumer's "Brand" (blaze) to "Band" (bond) in line 8 is unclear.

The poem takes the peculiar form of a conversation between a lover and his lovesick heart; the heart is realized musically in a virtuoso tenor part, while the rest of the quartet constitutes the interrogator.

The inclusion of minor subdominant and minor tonic harmonies in the seemingly lighthearted introduction signals the setting's characteristic blending of pathos with humor. Similar turns to the minor underscore the passion of the tenor's responses to the generally more diatonic (and cool-headed) questions; minor inflections also color his references to death (mm. 35–36 and 39–40) and his expressions of desire that he may soon perish (m. 74–end).

In m. 20 of the Peters edition, the F in the left hand of the accompaniment lacks a ♮ sign.

A representative example of subtle humor appears in the F-major episode. When the tenor responds in m. 45 to the query "What would you give to see her?" the pianist's left hand joins him in $\frac{3}{4}$ meter while the right hand sounds in $\frac{12}{16}$, both in contradiction to the prevailing $\frac{6}{8}$; the resulting chaos seems to prompt the others to chide, "You speak nonsense!"

Though the music modulates freely, the return of the tonic key and opening musical material in mm. 32 and 72 provides a sense of structure, contributing to the effect of rondo noted above. The sufferer's plight is treated with obvious sympathy, and despite the oddity of the situation, the piece is dramatically convincing. When an excellent tenor is available, its effectiveness in performance is assured.

Neue Liebeslieder

OPUS 65 (NEW SONGS OF LOVE)

Neue Liebeslieder. New Songs of Love. Waltzes translated into English by Mrs. Natalia Macfarren. Walzer für vier Singstimmen und Pianoforte zu vier Händen von Johannes Brahms (Waltzes for four solo voices and piano, four hands, by Johannes Brahms), Op. 65. Score and parts published in September 1875 by N. Simrock in Berlin; publication number 7670; German and English texts.

Dismayed at the misunderstandings caused by the term *ad libitum* in the title of the *Liebeslieder,* Op. 52, Brahms specified that it was not to appear in connection with the *Neue Liebeslieder,* so that the Op. 65 cycle would always be performed with the voices. Still, Simrock published a version for piano duet without voices as Op. 65a in April 1877; publication number 7707.

The final version of the *Neue Liebeslieder* dates from 1874 in Vienna and Rüschlikon, though portions were completed earlier.

The first performance took place on 8 May 1875 at a symphony concert in Karlsruhe's Museumssaal, when Johanna Schwartz, Luise Walter, Benedikt Kürner, and Josef Hauser sang nine waltzes from manuscript with Otto Dessoff and Brahms at the piano.

The texts of nos. 1–14 are translations from *Polydora, ein weltpoetisches Liederbuch* (Frankfurt am Main, 1855) by Georg Friedrich Daumer (1800–1875). The text of "Zum Schluß" is the concluding verse of the elegy *Alexis und Dora* by Johann Wolfgang von Goethe (1749–1832).

Waltzes 1–14 are in $\frac{3}{4}$ meter, and the opening instruction *Lebhaft, doch nicht schnell* (lively, but not fast) may be regarded as applying to the set as a whole. "Zum Schluß" is in $\frac{9}{4}$ and is marked *Ruhig* (quietly).

The approximate duration of the entire cycle is 18′30.

As with the Op. 52 *Liebeslieder,* the work seems to have been arranged in large subgroups of dances within a coherent whole. Here there are two groups of seven, plus an epilogue. Each group has a first and last movement for full quartet, enclosing not only another quartet but also four movements for solo voice or (in one case) duet; the concluding waltz of each group is in a form larger than the prevailing simple binary. The first group moves from A as tonic through D minor and F major to C; the second proceeds through E♭ major to G minor and major, and thence through E major back to A.

The $\frac{9}{4}$ Goethe setting "Zum Schluß" addresses "you Muses" and is in the form of a passacaglia interrupted by a contrapuntal central section. The key, F major, relates to the work's apparent tonic, A, as submediant—Brahms's usual choice for consideration of the unreal or imaginary. The weight of both form and text combine to lend the *New Songs of Love* substantially more gravity than is possessed by the earlier cycle.

Indeed, in comparison to the generally amiable *Liebeslieder,* the *Neue Liebeslieder* deal with darker, harsher emotions, among them dread, jealousy, rejection, lust, and despair. The two works complement, rather than duplicate, each other.

1.

Turkish

Verzicht', o Herz, auf Rettung,	Renounce rescue, O heart,
Dich wagend in der Liebe Meer!	when you venture on the sea of love!
Denn tausend Nachen schwimmen	For a thousand boats are floundering,
Zertrümmert am Gestad umher!	smashed upon the surrounding
	shore!

A minor; *Lebhaft, doch nicht schnell* (lively, but not fast); SATB.

Approximate duration: 0′45.
Binary.

The piano introduction announces both the high level of emotional energy and the contrary motion that characterize the movement. The Neapolitan harmony in m. 3 signals the anguish that underlies the text.

The initial vocal phrase introduces two important motives—the stepwise quarter notes in contrary motion of m. 5 and the dotted quarter followed by three eighths of m. 6. Aided by the *sforzando* in the piano, the phrase rises quickly to a climax on "o Herz." Its span of three measures is in effect stretched to four by the piano's repeated measure.

Four-measure phrases are in fact the norm, though phrase 4 joins two two-measure segments, and the final phrase seems lengthened by its interior hemiola.

The second part opens with a striking use of unison voices against a wavelike accompaniment based on the contrary-motion, quarter-note motive and bristling with accidentals. The *sforzandi* in the piano that illustrate the repeated "zertrümmert" recall the earlier one on "Herz" and reinforce Daumer's suggestion that the heart risks disaster on the sea of love.

2.

Persian

Moḥammad Shams Od-Dīn Ḥāfiẓ (c. 1326–c. 1390)

Finstere Schatten der Nacht,	Sinister shadows of the night,
Wogen und Wirbelgefahr!	waves and whirlpools' danger!
Sind wohl, die da gelind	Are those who gently
Rasten auf sicherem Lande,	rest on safe ground truly
Euch zu begreifen im Stande?	in a position to understand you?
Das ist der nur allein,	That can be done only by him
Welcher auf hoher See	who struggles on the high seas
Stürmischer Öde treibt,	in stormy solitude,
Meilen entfernt vom Strande.	miles away from shore.

A minor; SATB.

Approximate duration: 1'30.

Modified binary; A A' A'' B B.

This movement is related to that preceding not only by key but also by the poetic image of perilous seas and by musical material—the pair of phrases that open the second part, the harmonies of the piano postlude, and the restless, flowing eighth notes of the accompaniment all derive from the introduction of no. 1.

Though quieter than its predecessor, no. 2 acquires urgency from its prevailing three-measure phrase structure.

The initial period for bass alone is immediately repeated in a scoring for all four voices; the third statement has a three-measure insert—a transposed repetition of its first phrase in the key of the relative major.

Noteworthy in the second part are the paired voices at "Das ist der nur allein" and again at "Meilen entfernt vom Strande," the rising sequential treatment of "welcher auf hoher See" and "stürmischer Öde treibt," and the torrent of continuous eighth notes that seem to spiral down from top to bottom of the keyboard at the beginning and end of the section.

3.
Latvian-Lithuanian

An jeder Hand die Finger	I had decorated the fingers
Hatt' ich bedeckt mit Ringen,	of both hands with rings,
Die mir geschenkt mein Bruder	which my brother gave me
In seinem Liebessinn.	out of affection.
Und einen nach dem andern	And one after the other
Gab ich dem schönen, aber	I gave them away to the handsome but
Unwürdigen Jüngling hin.	unworthy young man.

A (or F) major; S.

Approximate duration: 1′15.
Binary.

At the suggestion of Otto Dessoff (the other pianist who took part in the first performance), who had reservations about the high tessitura of no. 3, Brahms wrote to Simrock on 16 June 1875 recommending its transposition into a lower key. Accordingly, a transposition into F major was printed as an appendix. The smooth progression of keys must have been one of Brahms's principal considerations—F is a full major third lower than A, but it is the first key in chromatic descent from A to bridge equally well the movement from the preceding A minor to the D minor that follows.

In mm. 4–5 (and 12–13) the piano *primo* briefly abandons its doubling of the voice to pursue its own quasi-sequential melody; a new left-hand part in mm. 10–12 treats the immediately preceding melodic motive in falling sequence, another level of which appears in mm. 14–16.

The second part shifts to the tonic minor and begins with a phrase that continues the idea of falling sequence in all parts. The piano counters with a rising sequence in mm. 21–22. Piano *primo* underscores the key word "unwürdigen" by trailing the voice canonically by a half beat in the left hand, a full beat in the right. "Jüngling hin" extends the vocal phrase to five measures, overlapping the cadence in the piano and the start of its new four-measure group.

The accompaniment of the repeated "dem Schönen," with its quarter notes in contrary motion and its *sforzando* chords, recalls the setting of the similarly repeated "zertrümmert" in no. 1 (the resemblance is particularly marked in the key of A because the harmonies are similar) and suggests symbolically that physical beauty is a prime source of potential destruction on the sea of love.

Together with the return of the tonic major, the opening phrase of the movement reappears in the piano as its final phrase; the soprano part contributes initial contrary-motion quarter notes before wending its independent way to the concluding tonic.

4.

Sicilian

Ihr schwarzen Augen,	You dark eyes,
Ihr dürft nur winken—	you need only wink—
Paläste fallen	palaces collapse
Und Städte sinken.	and cities decay.
Wie sollte steh'n	In such a struggle
In solchem Strauß	how could my heart
Mein Herz, von Karten	stand, that flimsy
Das schwache Haus?	house of cards?

D minor; B.

Approximate duration: 0′45.
Binary.

In all but the last of the four phrases the vocal melody eschews the upbeat beginnings of the piano. There is virtually no repetition in the vocal line after the rhythmic reiteration within the first phrase, but the rhythmic similarity of phrases 2, 3, and 4 in the piano provides counterbalancing stability.

Instances of musical metaphor include the lines that plunge on "fallen," fall less precipitously on "sinken," and descend gradually but inevitably on "von Karten das schwache Haus"; and the thorny cluster of dissonances that accumulates at "solchem Strauß."

5.
Russian

Wahre, wahre deinen Sohn,
  Nachbarin, vor Wehe,
Weil ich ihn mit schwarzem Aug'
  Zu bezaubern gehe.
	Protect, protect your son,
	  neighbor woman, from woe,
	because I am going to bewitch him
	  with my dark eyes.

O, wie brennt das Auge mir,
  Das zu zünden fodert!
Flammet ihm die Seele nicht—
  Deine Hütte lodert.
	Oh, how my eyes burn,
	  demanding to inflame him!
	If his soul does not ignite—
	  your cottage will burn.

D minor; A.

Approximate duration: 1′05.

Binary.

Like the linked movements 1 and 2, no. 5 is related to no. 4 by key, poetic imagery, and musical material. Here the uniting image is dark eyes hyperbolically endowed with supernatural power; the shared musical idea is the three-eighth-note upbeat that figures prominently in both.

The initial *sotto voce* three-note motive in the piano—a slur and two staccatos—sounds both ominous and stealthy. It reappears in the second part at "das zu zünden" and in the closing phrase at "deine Hütte lodert."

"Wehe" in m. 7 is illustrated by the vocal leap upward and the *sforzando* diminished-seventh chord in the accompaniment. The repeated augmented-second motive in the vocal line at "O, wie brennt das Auge mir" hints at the aching caused by desire. As though delving gradually deeper into the realm of imagination, the second part, at "das zu zünden fodert," moves from A major to its mediant, C♯ minor, then on to B major, the submediant of the tonic major—Brahms's two favored tonal relationships for the exploration of unreality.

"Flammet ihm die Seele nicht" is given a particularly dramatic setting. It begins like a higher sequential restatement of the earlier phrase with its augmented seconds. But the melodic line is diverted by mounting unease, marked by hemiola in the piano and a *crescendo.* As though pondering for the first time the possibility of failure, the singer repeats "die Seele nicht" within the span of a tritone, *forte,* and breaks off. A persistent, distressful diminished-seventh harmony recalls "Wehe" in m. 7 and attempts to wrest the tonal center back to the real world of D minor. Suddenly a long arpeggio, like a shriek of rage, begins in the top register of the piano; it traverses the diminished seventh chord and a dissonance-embellished dominant to arrive at the middle of the keyboard and the furtive staccato motive with which the movement began, the three-eighths upbeat figure now superimposed.

The vocal line is at last allowed to complete its sequence, but a half step higher rather than a whole step—"deine Hütte lodert" is set to the same melodic shape as the earlier "das zu zünden fodert."

6.

Spanish

Rosen steckt mir an die Mutter,	My mother pins roses on me
Weil ich gar so trübe bin.	because I am so melancholy.
Sie hat Recht, die Rose sinket,	She is right; the rose withers,
So, wie ich, entblättert hin.	thus robbed, like me, of its petals.

F major; S.

Approximate duration: 0′45.
Binary.
The simple setting affectingly reflects the sadness of the terse text. The vocal line is filled with rests, even midword, that suggest sobbing intakes of breath. The first part reaches a cadence not on the dominant (C) as expected but rather on the mediant (A minor/major, the relative of C). The last part borrows so freely from F minor that the final major chord sounds like a *tierce de Picardie.*

An effect of broadening in the closing bars is created by hemiola in the accompaniment.

7.

Russian-Polish Dance Song

Vom Gebirge, Well' auf Well',	From the mountains, wave after wave,
Kommen Regengüsse,	come downpours of rain,
Und ich gäbe dir so gern	and I would love to shower you with
Hunderttausend Küsse.	a hundred thousand kisses.

C major; *Lebhaft* (lively); SATB.

Approximate duration: 1′10.

Rounded binary. The second part includes a return of the opening material and repetition of the entire text.

Several elements in addition to its larger form and jubilant tone contribute to the effectiveness of this movement as a conclusion for the first large group of dances in the cycle. A motive in contrary-motion quarter notes, which seems calculated to recall the similar motive in no. 1, begins both periods of the first part and constitutes nearly all of the contrasting material in the second part. Further, the other keys emphasized are more often the A minor/major and near relatives of the earlier movements than the expected dominant or subdominant of C.

There is an effective use of the voices in unison (again recalling no. 1) for the opening theme and again at its reappearance. A particular source of delight to the listener is the ambivalent metric structure, as exemplified by the three settings of the poem's first couplet: in mm. 9–16, each line clearly occupies a four-measure phrase; in the apparently similar structure preceding, the voices have phrases of four and three measures instead, having left the first measure to the piano alone; at the restatement near the end, the two lines seem to occupy only five measures plus an extended upbeat. Additional aural confusion results from what are heard as elisions, such as the piano's apparent phrase-beginning in m. 24 as the voices sing "Küsse" to complete their phrase, or the two-measure piano hemiola that bridges the concluding pair of four-measure vocal phrases. The overall effect is the evocation of a kind of joyous delirium, matching that of the poet.

8.

Russian-Polish Dance Song

Weiche Gräser im Revier,	Soft grasses in the district,
Schöne stille Plätzchen—	beautiful, quiet little nooks—
O, wie linde ruht es hier	Oh, how pleasantly one can rest here
Sich mit einem Schätzchen!	with a sweetheart!

E♭ major; *Ruhig* (quietly); SATB.

Approximate duration: 1′25.

Binary; A A′ B B.

The second half of the cycle begins with a gentle pastorale that contrasts sharply with its boisterous predecessor.

The first section features a placid melody in the piano, the four voices providing an accompaniment made up mostly of rest-separated chords. The repetition gives one melody phrase each to the soprano and tenor and adds octave doubling and a pizzicato bass in the piano.

The second part contains more conventional homophonic writing for the voices. The alto and tenor are doubled in the piano's middle register; the rhythms of the soprano line, but seldom its pitches, are duplicated by the piano treble.

The three scalar quarter notes that constituted an important unifying motive in the first group of dances again figure prominently, though the element of contrary motion appears as linear contrast rather than simultaneously. The melody of the first part is based entirely on the downward movement of the motive, while the tiny introduction and the bridges between phrases reverse the direction. Conversely, the upward direction of the piano melody in the tender sequences that open the second part is countered immediately by two successive appearances of the motive moving downward.

9.

Polish

Nagen am Herzen	I feel a poison
Fühl' ich ein Gift mir.	gnawing at my heart.
Kann sich ein Mädchen,	Can a maiden
Ohne zu fröhnen	conceive of living
Zärtlichem Hang,	her entire life
Fassen ein ganzes	deprived of rapture,
Wonneberaubtes	without indulging her
Leben entlang?	tender inclinations?

G minor; S.

Approximate duration: 1′05.

Rounded binary.

The doleful key of G minor here, with its sighing accompaniment, proceeds easily from the related E♭ major preceding.

The scalar-quarter-note motive again plays a prominent role, now set back a beat rather than lying within the measure. It appears in piano *primo* in single occurrences at the start and in sequentially conjoined pairs at the beginning of the second part. Hemiola in the last few measures causes the motive to sound in augmentation in the final notes of the voice and *primo* right hand, answered in free canon by the left hand.

At the return of opening material at "fassen ein ganzes," the piano not only recalls the quarter-note motive but also refers to the rhythm in eighth notes that began no. 4—is it the thought of a pair of dark eyes that causes the maiden's self-doubt?

Other metaphoric constructions are more forthright. At "ohne zu fröhnen zärtlichem Hang" (without indulging her tender inclinations), there is a modulation to the Neapolitan, Brahms's key of pathos, with "zärtlichem" harmonized by major, then minor, subdominant, his symbol for increasingly compassionate tenderness. The chromatic lines and sequences that underlie "ein ganzes, ganzes wonneberaubtes" suggest the painful prospect of a life deprived of rapture, and the closing augmentation with its trailing canon illustrates the protractedness of such a life.

10.

Malayan

Ich kose süß mit der und der	I sweetly caress this girl and that,
Und werde still und kranke;	and become quiet and suffer,
Denn ewig, ewig kehrt zu dir,	because always, always my thoughts
O Nonna, mein Gedanke!	return to you, O Nonna!

G major; T.

Approximate duration: 1′05.

Binary.

Frequent diminished-seventh harmonies and chromatic borrowings tinge the prevailing major mode with minor plaintiveness.

The two phrases of the first part are freely sequential. The first moves to a cadence on the tonic; the second, on the dominant. Both begin with a diminished-seventh chord, *sforzando,* and become quieter as they progress toward less ambiguous harmonies. Both contrast two measures of $\frac{3}{4}$ with a two-measure hemiola.

In the second part, the sound of free sequence relates mm. 9–10 to mm. 11–12, both pairs beginning with a *sforzando* diminished-seventh chord, and mm. 15–16 to mm. 17–18, both of which diminish as they progress. Hemiola recurs in mm. 19–20.

A rhythmic figure comprising a dotted quarter and three eighths is important, appearing in the piano or the vocal line (or both) in twelve of the movement's twenty-two measures. The motive recalls the similar one in nos. 4 and 5, but here, with the sole exception of the first ending of the second part, the three eighth notes always descend, and they rarely function as an upbeat.

In the Peters edition, the ♮ signs are missing from the downbeat Fs in piano *primo* in m. 4 of the second part.

11.

Polish

Alles, alles in den Wind	Everything, everything you say to me
Sagst du mir, du Schmeichler!	is in vain, you flatterer!
Allesamt verloren sind	Your efforts are altogether
Deine Müh'n, du Heuchler!	lost, you hypocrite!
Einem andern Fang' zu lieb	Set your trap for
Stelle deine Falle!	some other prey instead!
Denn du bist ein loser Dieb,	Because you are a wanton thief,
Denn du buhlst um alle!	because you woo everyone!

G major; *Lebhaft* (lively); S.

Approximate duration: 0′55.
Binary.

No. 11 is closely related to no. 10—in fact, the same progression of harmonies makes up the first parts of both—though the dotted quarter– three eighths motive is lacking. Both four-measure phrases of the first part begin with a *sforzando* diminished-seventh chord and contrast two measures of $\frac{3}{4}$ with a two-measure hemiola; both six-measure phrases of the second part begin with a *sforzando* diminished-seventh chord and contrast four measures of $\frac{3}{4}$ with a two-measure hemiola. Though the melodies and harmonies differ, within each pair of phrases the rhythms in all parts are identical, suggesting the free sequences of no. 10.

All four phrases end with a *forte* punctuation consisting of two staccato quarter-note chords.

The frequently shifting rhythms, strong dynamic contrasts, and turbulent accompanying eighth notes combine to lend an appropriately waspish tone.

12.

Serbian

Schwarzer Wald, dein Schatten ist so düster!	Dark forest, your shade is so gloomy!
Armes Herz, dein Leiden ist so drückend!	Poor heart, your sorrow is so oppressive!
Was dir einzig wert, es steht vor Augen;	The only thing you treasure stands before your eyes;
Ewig untersagt ist Huldvereinung.	blessed union is forbidden forever.

G minor; SATB.

Approximate duration: 1′35.
Binary.

Brahms later added the indication *Lebhaft* (lively) to nos. 12–14 in his own copy of the first edition, which omitted it; the printers apparently assumed that its appearance in no. 11 would continue to affect the ensuing movements.

The impassioned setting is given an aura of ardor by its many long appoggiaturas and a layer of unrest by the conflicting hemiola that occurs in piano *primo; secondo* has hemiola rarely, the voices, never.

The second part introduces a simpler accompaniment and the major mode at "Was dir einzig wert," but a *crescendo* leads through "es steht vor Augen" to a *forte* at "Augen," poignant Neapolitan harmony, and the return of hemiola. The closing phrase is constructed similarly, but "ewig untersagt" demands harmonization with minor rather than major. The climactic moment of the movement is the *forte* "Huldvereinung," which prompts a reference in the piano to its opening melody; the fervor of a sonorous diminished-seventh chord gradually recedes in the postlude through a dissonance-laden minor subdominant to a resigned tonic major.

13.
Russian

Nein, Geliebter, setze dich
    Mir so nahe nicht!
Starre nicht so brünstiglich
    Mir in's Angesicht.
	No, beloved, don't sit
	    so close to me!
	Don't gaze into my face
	    so ardently.

Wie es auch im Busen brennt,
    Dämpfe deinen Trieb,
Daß es nicht die Welt erkennt,
    Wie wir uns so lieb!
	Even though it burns in your breast,
	    stifle your desire,
	so that the world doesn't realize
	    how much in love we are!

E major; SA.

Approximate duration: 1′15.
Rounded binary.

In his own copy of the first edition, Brahms later added the indication "Lebhaft" (lively). Mandyczewski, in his editorial commentary for the Breitkopf & Härtel complete edition, remarks that if one wished to emulate Brahms's own style of performing the movement, he should write in "Sehr lebhaft und heimlich" (very lively and secretively).

The initial octave E implies the relative minor of the preceding G major, but gradually the hushed warmth of E major accumulates. Prevalent pedal points and minimal harmonic activity add to a sense of suspended time—the first part abandons its E pedal only to make a cadence on the dominant.

The eighth-note melody found in mm. 3–4 in piano *secondo* forms the basis of the contrasting music in the second part. Two measures each of C♯ major, G♯ minor, and D♯ major harmonize the *crescendo* to *forte* of "wie es auch im Busen brennt," and two each on B and E accompany the *decrescendo* to *pianissimo* of "dämpfe deinen Trieb."

Upon its return the opening music again forsakes its pedal point only to form a cadence, this time on the tonic.

The score conceals a waggish comment from the composer. Of all of the *Liebeslieder,* only this frequently requires *primo*'s left hand to play lower on the keyboard than *secondo*'s right hand. For the two pianists, as presumably for the lovers of the text, sitting close is not optional but necessary!

14.
Russian

Flammenauge, dunkles Haar,
Knabe wonnig und verwogen!
Kummer ist durch dich hinein
In mein armes Herz gezogen.

Kann in Eis der Sonne Brand,
Sich in Nacht der Tag verkehren?
Kann die heiße Menschenbrust
Atmen ohne Glutbegehren?

Ist die Flur so voller Licht,
Daß die Blum' im Dunkel stehe?

Ist die Welt so voller Lust,
Daß das Herz in Qual vergehe?

Flaming eyes, dark hair,
delightful and bold boy!
Sorrow is drawn through you
right into my poor heart.

Can the sun's flame change into ice,
or the day into night?
Can the hot human breast
breathe without the glow of desire?

When the field is so full of light,
why should the blossom stand in the
dark?

When the world is so full of joy,
why should the heart be lost in
suffering?

A minor/major; SATB.

Approximate duration: 1'45.

The form resembles a large binary structure with coda but includes elements of through-composition.

In his own copy of the first edition, Brahms added the indication "Lebhaft" (lively).

The last of the waltzes proper returns to the key and vivacity of the first movement of the cycle. Appropriate to its male-directed text, the opening section is sung by the female voices only. Most of the melodic material for both the voices and the piano uses hemiola, whose conflict with the regular $\frac{3}{4}$ of the accompaniment underlines the inner turmoil expressed by the poem.

Beginning in m. 10, the pianists have a derivative of their opening melody, first in inversion, then transposed into B♭ minor. The voices have a skeletal version of the same melody in canon at the distance of two measures; at the same time the pianists have a canon only one measure apart, and the overlapping hemiola patterns that result produce additional unrest. After some curious telescoping in mm. 17–18, *secondo* emerges as the leader in another canon separated by only one beat during the retransition to the return of opening material and text in m. 22.

The repetition of stanza 1 begins like a somewhat more elaborate reprise but is soon transformed into an extended transition to A major. Neapolitan and diminished-seventh harmonies are prominent, evoking the "sorrow" of the text.

All four voices join in the A-major music, which constitutes the repeated second part of the quasi-binary structure. At the repetition the tenor is given the first phrase of melody, which is answered in inversion by the alto; the other voices accumulate contrapuntally to a full homophonic texture for the last two lines of text.

The eighth notes in the A-major piano melody derive from the beginning of the movement, but their downward spirals also recall the important eighth-note patterns in movements 1 and 2. Four-note groupings hint at the hemiola that was so pervasive in the first part of the movement. At the repetition the alternation of registers is reversed.

The vocal melody in quarter notes at "ohne Glutbegehren" is twice repeated by the piano in downward sequence to effect the transition between verses. The same melody at the end (at "Herz in Qual vergehe") is again taken up by the piano. In *forte* it leads to a descending arpeggio on second-inversion tonic, in *piano,* to a quiet conclusion on tonic in root position.

[15.]
Zum Schluß (Conclusion)

Text by Johann Wolfgang von Goethe (1749–1832)

Nun, Ihr Musen, genug! Vergebens strebt ihr zu schildern, Wie sich Jammer und Glück wechseln in liebender Brust. Heilen könnet die Wunden ihr nicht, die Amor geschlagen; Aber Linderung kommt einzig, ihr Guten, von euch.	Now you Muses, enough! In vain you struggle to describe how misery and gladness alternate in the loving breast. You cannot heal the wounds inflicted by Cupid; but relief comes only, you kind-hearted ones, from you.

F major; $^9_4$; *Ruhig* (quietly); SATB.

Approximate duration: 2′25.

Passacaglia, interrupted by a central section in imitative counterpoint. The six pitches that make up the ground bass correspond to the six-note melody that opens the concluding prayer for the healing of heartache (also by Goethe) in the Alto Rhapsody, Op. 59.

Brahms's parenthetical $\frac{3}{4}$ implies that the primary $\frac{9}{4}$ meter is more a recognition of the poem's twice-triple meter than a radical departure from the prevailing waltz tempo. The character of dance, however, yields to that of epilogue—already in the first measure, the lilt of the waltz is contradicted by ties across strong beats and *secondo*'s grouping of eighth notes into threes, in effect suggesting a duple meter.

In addition to the ground bass, four complete statements of which form the basis of the first section, the introduction presents a melody that reappears as transition to the next section and whose opening rising triad outline (an augmentation of the accompaniment figure in *secondo*) becomes important in the coda.

The voices enter in midstatement of the ground. After their homophonic evocation of the muses, a contrapuntal texture predominates until near the end of the section. Despite the restrictions imposed by the ostinato, the harmonies touch both F minor and B♭ minor.

The transition to D♭ major occurs over a bass pedal F, but a half-statement of the ground is heard in the tenor register of the piano.

The new section has three important contrapuntal elements, all treated in free canon: the triad-outlining setting of "Heilen könnet die Wunden ihr nicht," with its initial rising fourth; the mostly stepwise "die Amor geschlagen," marked by the scalar descent beginning at "Amor"; and the piano motive comprising a rising eighth-note arpeggio followed by falling quarter notes. As the voices come together in homophony at the end of the section, the piano becomes silent, leaving the cadence to the voices alone. "Geschlagen" (inflicted) is represented in three dissonant settings of decreasing acerbity: a combined suspension and diminished-seventh chord, *sforzando,* marks the soprano's singing of the word in *forte* in m. 15; for the male voices later in the same measure, it is harmonized by successive minor- and dominant-seventh chords; its appearance unaccompanied and *piano* in m. 17 prompts a prolonged 4–3 suspension against inner-voice passing and neighboring tones, all resolving satisfyingly into the resumption of the passacaglia.

Four more statements of the ground bass underlie the remainder of the movement, two each in the left and right hand of *secondo.* The voices are given a melody recalling that in m. 5, and they soon rise to a *forte* A-major climax at "einzig" in m. 21.

The tranquil coda, over a bass pedal F, has statements of the six-note ostinato melody in each of the four voices in turn—bass, tenor, soprano, and alto. Piano *primo* interjects its rising-triad-outline motive in gentle octaves, finally adding a repeated rising scalar third; the composite gesture seems to symbolize the awakening of hope for the healing of the afflictions induced by Love.

Five Duets for Soprano and Alto

OPUS 66

The title page reads like that of the Op. 61 duets, *Duette für Sopran und Alt mit Begleitung des Pianoforte von Johannes Brahms* (Duets for soprano and alto with piano accompaniment by Johannes Brahms), but includes the notice "Translated into English by Mrs. Natalia Macfarren" and a listing of the contents of Opp. 20, 61, and 66 with their text incipits. The score and parts of the five Op. 66 duets were printed in October/November 1875 by N. Simrock in Berlin; publication numbers 7703 (score) and 7704 (parts); German text only. Subsequent printings included texts in both German and English.

Brahms very much disliked the appearance of the added English in printed song texts. In fact, even after his growing popularity in England made it commercially desirable to publish in both languages, Simrock customarily made a small initial printing in German only for the use of Brahms and his friends.

In four of these five duets, as in the four of Op. 61, Brahms avoids dialogue texts with their inherent theatricality—"Jägerlied" is the sole exception. But here, even more than in the earlier set, a new kind of drama becomes apparent, deriving from the combination of emotional sincerity, terseness of expression, and the attempt to portray the text's changing moods in minute detail—now even the use of canon is likely to have metaphoric significance. (The same aura of honesty and empathy is typical also of Brahms's solo song composition from the early 1870s onward.) The dramatic conviction results from the universality with which the situation is depicted rather than from the clash of conflicting viewpoints.

Klänge I, Op. 66/1 (Sounds, no. 1)

Text by Klaus Groth (1819–1899)

Aus der Erde quellen Blumen,	Flowers spring from the earth,
Aus der Sonne quillt das Licht,	light flows from the sun,
Aus dem Herzen quillt die Liebe,	love emanates from the heart,
Und der Schmerz, der es zerbricht.	as does the sorrow that breaks it.
Und die Blumen müssen welken,	And flowers must wither,
Und dem Lichte folgt die Nacht,	and night follows daylight,
Und der Liebe folgt das Sehnen,	and love is followed by longing,
Das das Herz so düster macht.	that makes the heart so disconsolate.

G minor; $\frac{2}{4}$; *Andante;* SA.

Approximate duration: 1′40.

Varied strophic.

The composition date is uncertain, but Groth received manuscript copies of both "Klänge I" and "Klänge II" for his birthday on 24 April 1875.

The first performance is not documented.

The text is from *Hundert Blätter, Paralipomena zum Quickborn* (Hamburg, 1854).

The two "Klänge" settings constitute a double elegy on the death of love, the second somewhat more wide-ranging emotionally than the first. While each is complete in itself, they may well have been intended for paired performance; the meter and tempo are the same, and the turn to G major at the end of no. 1 provides a B♮ to function as a bridge to the B minor of no. 2.

The two stanzas of the poem deal with opposites—the first with growth, light, and love; the second with decay, darkness, and yearning. Brahms's setting provides a musical metaphor for each, primarily through the relationship between the two voices.

In strophe 1, the alto moves synchronously and in concord with the soprano. Harmonic movement in the piano transforms the tied notes of mm. 12–13 into dissonances symbolic of "der Schmerz."

In strophe 2, the soprano melody is restated, somewhat extended, but an entirely new alto part imitates throughout in strict canon by inversion, starting a fifth below and one beat later—a vivid reminder (visual, if not always aural) that every relevant natural process is followed by its antithesis just as is each phrase of the melody.

The knell-like introduction to each strophe trails off into silence. Its more sonorous variant as postlude seems to portray both intense yearning and the moroseness which, oddly, the change to major of the tonic harmony engenders.

Klänge II, Op. 66/2 (Sounds, no. 2)
Text by Klaus Groth (1819–1899)

Wenn ein müder Leib begraben,	When a spent body is buried,
Klingen Glocken ihn zur Ruh',	bells ring it to its rest,
Und die Erde schließt die Wunde	and the earth closes the wound
Mit den schönsten Blumen zu!	with the most beautiful flowers!
Wenn die Liebe wird begraben,	When love is buried,
Singen Lieder sie zur Ruh',	songs sing it to its rest,
Und die Wunde bringt die Blumen,	and the wound produces flowers,
Doch das Grab erst schließt sie zu!	though only the grave heals it!

B minor; $\frac{2}{4}$; *Andante;* SA.

Approximate duration: 2'05.

A hybrid form with characteristics of both strophic variation and through-composition.

The date of composition is uncertain, but Brahms sent manuscript copies of both "Klänge I" and "Klänge II" to Groth for his birthday on 24 April 1875.

The first performance is not documented.

The text is from *Hundert Blätter, Paralipomena zum Quickborn* (Hamburg, 1854).

The setting is based on the opening motive of the *Minnelied* "Mir ist Leide," which is also the theme of the slow movement variations of Brahms's F♯-minor piano sonata, Op. 2. Since the *Minnelied* deals with the pain resulting from the departure of an unattainable beloved of "very high station," and since the sonata is strongly associated with Brahms's first visit to the Schumanns, in 1853—it is, in fact, dedicated to Clara Schumann—many commentators have conjectured that "Klänge II" reflects some sad connection with the Schumann family. But Robert's death had occurred some twenty years earlier, and Clara remained the treasured confidante she had always been (though their relationship had become strained in the late 1860s). The most likely source of Schumann sorrow would seem to be the relatively recent death in 1872 of daughter Julie, for whom Brahms had felt devout, if unexpressed, affection, and whose betrothal and subsequent marriage in 1869 had caused him considerable anguish. Whatever its inspiration, the setting is affecting and deeply felt, full of unexpected chromatic alterations and poignant dissonances.

Because it is likely to escape the ear, one notes with some surprise that the piano bass imitates the first nine notes of the first vocal phrase and the first four notes of the second in canon by augmentation. At "mit den schönsten Blumen" in m. 13, the soprano line blossoms into a new broken-chord figure in sixteenth notes, which is imitated by the piano in m. 14 and by the alto voice in m. 15.

The piano interlude sustains the dominant to which the strophe has modulated but allows the emotional tension to abate. Its melodic material is a twice-heard twining figure in sixteenth notes, based on the initial "Mir ist Leide" motive with its distinctive diminished fourth.

Over a dominant pedal, the second strophe begins with the same melody as the first, a step higher; at "begraben" the voices are becalmed in diminished-seventh harmony while a right-hand arpeggio sinks into the piano's low register. The hushed, prolonged Neapolitan harmony at "singen Lieder sie zur Ruh'" is arresting (one of the most striking features of "Mir ist Leide" as it appears in the Op. 2 sonata is a turn to the Neapolitan in m. 5); the broken-chord figure that seemed to illustrate "Blumen" in strophe 1 here represents "Lieder," and at the second "zur Ruh'" it broadens to eighth notes and a near cessation of motion at the cadence on the dominant. "Und die Wunde bringt die Blumen" brings the return of the opening melody in the key of the tonic, and again the piano bass imitates in augmentation. But the closing line ("doch das Grab . . .") begins in the alto with a symbolic inversion of the principal motive, emphasized by the soprano's imitation a sixth above. Quickly the phrase rises to *forte* and a climactic cadence punctuated by two clashing suspensions.

Using the same repeated twining figure as the earlier interlude, the piano postlude soars above the voices to begin its long descent, touchingly alternating tonic-major harmonies with the wistful sound of the minor subdominant.

Am Strande, Op. 66/3 (On the shore)
Text by Hermann Hölty (1828–1887)

Es sprechen und blicken die Wellen	The waves speak and look,
Mit sanfter Stimme, mit freundlichem Blick,	with soft voice, with friendly glance,
Und wiegen die träumende Seele	and lull the dreaming soul
In ferne Tage zurück.	back to bygone days.

Aus fernen verklungenen Tagen	From distant, faded days
Spricht's heimlich mit sanften	gentle voices address me furtively,
Stimmen zu mir,	
Schaut's heimlich mit freundlichen	a friendly gaze furtively observes
Blicken	
Zum Wandrer am Strande hier.	the wanderer here on the shore.
Mir ist, als hätten die Stimmen,	It seems to me as if the voices,
Die je die Seele mir sanft bewegt,	which always gently stirred my soul,
Und alle die freundlichen Blicke	and all the friendly glances
Sich in die Wellen gelegt.	had reposed themselves in the
	waves.

E♭ major; common time; *Ruhig* (quietly); SA.

Approximate duration: 2'10.

Ternary form (A B A).

Composed during summer 1875 at Ziegelhausen, near Heidelberg.

The first performance took place on 13 March 1882 at a Richard Dannenberg recital in Hamburg, sung by Dannenberg and Fräulein Gowa.

The text is from *Bilder und Balladen,* of which Brahms owned the 1872 Hanover edition; a second, enlarged edition appeared in 1874. Hermann Hölty was a Hamburg theologian, the grandnephew of one of Brahms's favorite poets, Ludwig Hölty.

Though the text is somewhat obscure, the setting is straightforward and personal. The gracefully flowing melodic materials make use of even eighth notes over an accompaniment of triplets, and, excepting the stretched last phrase of the middle section, the music proceeds in four-measure segments.

The basic accompaniment figure—half-measure harmonies broken into triplets—is yet another example of Brahms's seemingly inexhaustible reserve of evocations of the motion of waves. The piano's only melodic contribution to the principal strophe is an arch bridging the second and third phrases (mm. 11–12), which strikes the ear as related to the soprano's "ferne" in m. 10.

The emphasis that this melodic flourish adds to the word "ferne" is only one of several examples of the important role played in the piece by the concept of remoteness. The third phrase not only derives its text from repetition of "in ferne Tage zurück" but itself repeats "ferne Tage." The immediate turn from tonic major to tonic minor at the end of the strophe opens the door to the distant keys to which the central section travels, including the "poignant" Neapolitan and the "imaginary world" lowered submediant. Even the canonic construction (into which the piano attempts to enter in mm. 20–23) is a literal representation of distance, both of pitch and of time. As the music of the piano's introduction reappears under the broadened final words "am Strande hier" to lead the way from dominant to tonic for the third strophe, one realizes in retrospect that its seeming wrong-key beginning was also a metaphor, originating elsewhere to arrive at the true tonic key.

As postlude, the same transitional music now leads from tonic to subdominant, whose lowered third and lengthening as it leads toward the plagal cadence reflect the poem's aura of nostalgia.

Jägerlied, Op. 66/4 (Huntsman's song)
Text by Karl Candidus (1817–1872)

Jäger, was jagst du die Häselein—	Huntsman, why do you hunt the young hare—
Die Häselein?	the young hare?
Häselein jag' ich, das muß so sein—	I hunt the young hare, it must be so—
Das muß so sein.	it must be so.
Jäger, was steht dir im Auge dein—	Huntsman, what is in your eyes—
Im Auge dein?	in your eyes?
Tränen wohl sind es, das muß so sein—	Perhaps it's tears, it must be so—
Das muß so sein!	it must be so!
Jäger, was hast du im Herzelein—	Huntsman, what have you in your heart—
Im Herzelein?	in your heart?
Liebe und Leiden, das muß so sein—	Love and sorrow, it must be so—
Das muß so sein.	it must be so.
Jäger, wann holst du dein Liebchen heim—	Hunstman, when will you fetch your sweetheart home—
Dein Liebchen heim?	your sweetheart home?
Nimmer, ach nimmer, das muß so sein—	Never, alas, never, it must be so—
Das muß so sein!	it must be so!

C major/minor; $\frac{2}{4}$/$\frac{6}{8}$; *Lebhaft* (lively); SA.

Approximate duration: 1′08.
Varied (double) strophic.
Composed during summer 1875 at Ziegelhausen, near Heidelberg.

The first performance is not documented.

The text is found in the poet's *Vermischte Gedichte* (Leipzig, 1969).

"Jägerlied," the only dialogue song in the opus, is cast in folkish question-and-answer form; the voices never sing together. The setting is one of the many of Brahms that progress from seeming folkloric naiveté at the outset to an intensely emotional climax.

The soprano asks her four questions *sempre più dolce* to virtually identical melodies in C major and $\frac{2}{4}$ meter (though a background rhythm of triplets is pervasive). The accompaniment is slightly varied for the second, but becomes markedly and progressively quieter rhythmically for the more personal third and fourth. The first three inquiries occur over a dominant pedal in the bass, which the fourth exchanges for chromatic movement downward, hinting at encroaching grief.

The alto huntsman's responses are in C minor and $\frac{6}{8}$, and their accompaniment is replete with the obligatory horn fifths. The first two are sung to the same three short phrases, the first of which is imitated in canon by the right hand and (abbreviated) a beat later by the left. But as the third and fourth replies become more impassioned and more desperate, the first and third phrases are altered accordingly. The first trades its stepwise movement for skips and its *piano* for *forte;* its register rises, and its accompaniment, now in urgent converging arpeggios, ranges farther afield harmonically. The third phrase, which originally lay within the interval of a third and spanned two measures, is now expanded to the range of a fifth and stretched to four measures in strophe 3, five measures in strophe 4. The dotted rhythm introduced in the piano part of strophe 3 grows in complexity in strophe 4 to become a $\frac{3}{4}$ dotted rhythm in the right hand against the prevailing $\frac{6}{8}$ in the left. Sighing horn fifths underlie the last few words and fade hesitantly to sad silence.

The text specifies neither the identity of the questioner nor the reason for the huntsman's tears. The increasingly anguished tone of the musical setting suggests that the dialogue is with the huntsman's own inner voice and that his sweetheart is dead, perhaps even killed, accidentally or not, by the huntsman himself.

Hüt' du dich! Op. 66/5 (Watch out!)

Text from Des Knaben Wunderhorn

Ich weiß ein Mäd'lein hübsch und fein,	I know a pretty and graceful lass,
Hüt' du dich!	watch out!
Es kann wohl falsch und freundlich sein,	She can be both false and friendly,

Hüt' du dich! Hüt' du dich!	watch out! watch out!
Vertrau' ihr nicht, sie narret dich.	Don't trust her, she'll fool you.

Sie hat zwei Äuglein, die sind
        braun,
Hüt' du dich!
Sie werden dich verliebt anschau'n,
Hüt' du dich! Hüt' du dich!
Vertrau' ihr nicht, sie narret dich.

She has two little eyes, they are
        brown,
watch out!
They will look at you amorously,
watch out! watch out!
Don't trust her, she'll fool you.

Sie hat ein lichtgoldfarb'nes Haar,
Hüt' du dich!
Und was sie red't, das ist nicht wahr,
Hüt' du dich! Hüt' du dich!
Vertrau' ihr nicht, sie narret dich.

She has light gold-colored hair,
watch out!
And what she says is not true,
watch out! watch out!
Don't trust her, she'll fool you.

Sie hat zwei Brüstlein, die sind
        weiß,
Hüt' du dich!
Sie legt's hervor mit allem Fleiß!
Hüt' du dich! Hüt' du dich!
Vertrau' ihr nicht, sie narret dich.

She has two little breasts, they are
        white,
watch out!
She lets them show on purpose!
Watch out! watch out!
Don't trust her, she'll fool you.

Sie gibt dir'n Kränzlein fein
        gemacht,
Hüt' du dich!
Für einen Narr'n wirst du geacht'!
Hüt' du dich! Hüt' du dich!
Vertrau' ihr nicht, sie narret dich.

She'll give you a finely made
        garland,
watch out!
You'll be regarded as a buffoon!
Watch out! watch out!
Don't trust her, she'll fool you.

B♭ major; $\frac{2}{4}$; *Lebhaft, heimlich und schalkhaft* (lively, secretively, and roguishly); SA.

Approximate duration: 1′10.
Strophic.

The composition is listed in an entry for December 1873 in Brahms's pocket calendar; a later handwritten notation for summer 1875 in his catalog of works probably refers to the final readying for publication.

Adolf Ritter von Schultner, tenor, and Adolf Wallnöfer, bass, sang the first public performance as part of a "Brahms-Abend" in Vienna on 24 April 1880. There had been an earlier private hearing on 29 January 1878 at Billroth's house.

The text is very old, dating back to the sixteenth century, when it ap-

peared in Berg and Newber's *68 Lieder* (Nuremberg, 1542). Friedrich Nico-
lai included it, with a new melody by Johann Friedrich Reichardt, in his *Ein
feyner kleyner Almanach* (Berlin-Stettin, 1777–1778). There is even an
English-language version by Longfellow, "I know a maiden fair to see."
Brahms used the poem as printed by Achim von Arnim and Clemens Brentano in *Des Knaben Wunderhorn* (Heidelberg, 1806–08). In verse 1, he
changed the *Wunderhorn's* "Maidlein" to "Mäd'lein"; in verse 2, "über-
zwerch anschau'n" to "verliebt anschau'n"; and in verse 4, "nach ihrem
Fleiß" to "mit allem Fleiß."

The voice parts are the same for the five strophes; the accompaniment
is somewhat more elaborate for strophes 2–5 than for strophe 1.

There are two important motives: the rising melodic skips (including
at least one fourth) with which the piano introduction ends and the soprano part begins; and the quarter-note rhythm that sets the reiterated
"hüt' du dich!" in mm. 9–12 and mm. 22–26—coupled in the latter case
with a falling melodic fourth.

The first, third, and sixth vocal phrases begin with the same rising-skip
motive in the tonic; two variants make up phrase 4, and a further leap
upward in phrase 6 caps the strophe with a high G. The original motive in
the key of the dominant appears in the piano to accompany phrase 2, the
first "hüt' du dich!" pair.

The quarter-note motive, with its falling fourth, recurs unexpectedly in
the piano in m. 21, overlapping the five-measure phrase 4 to begin the
series of falling imitations that make up the six-measure phrase 5. In strophes 2–5 the motive continues in the piano to accompany phrase 6.

The music with which the piano introduces each strophe reappears
as postlude, with a dominant-tonic cadence on successive staccato upbeats
amusingly appended.

The setting exemplifies the Brahmsian union of folk art with art song.
The text offers a warning born of folk wisdom, but it cannot be taken seri-
ously when clothed in such lighthearted music.

Four Ballads and Romances
for Two Voices

OPUS 75

Seinem Freunde Julius Allgeyer zugeeignet. Balladen und Romanzen für zwei Singstimmen mit Pianoforte von Johannes Brahms (Dedicated to his friend Julius Allgeyer. Ballads and romances for two solo voices with piano by Johannes Brahms), Op. 75. Score and parts published in November/December 1878 by N. Simrock in Berlin; publication numbers 8052 (score) and 8053 (parts); German only. An edition in both German and English (translated by Natalia Macfarren) appeared shortly after the initial printing.

Brahms first met the engraver and photographer Julius Allgeyer (1829–1900) in Düsseldorf in 1853, and they were lifelong close friends. Allgeyer was an enthusiastic supporter of both Brahms's music and the painting of their mutual friend Anselm Feuerbach (1829–1880); a critical biography of Feuerbach was his most important work.

Originally Brahms had intended to dedicate this work to Elisabeth von Herzogenberg, but he decided that the contents were inappropriate. As he wrote to Simrock on 12 September 1878, "Numbers 1 and 4 are too gruesome and numbers 2 and 3 too free for a lady." Elisabeth wrote to Brahms on 24 November 1879, in the playful tone she often used with him, "When shall I receive the something dedicated to me, which is my due after ignominiously relinquishing the other to Herr Allgeyer? I call it base to promise anyone such a Christmas present and then snatch it away again." A year later, in 1880, he dedicated the two piano rhapsodies, Op. 79, to her.

The Op. 75 ballads and romances are the most important and "biggest" of Brahms's compositions for two voices and piano, and they achieve a new level of emotional intensity. They therefore constitute a culmination not only of Brahms's contribution but of the entire genre.

The texts are all of the dialogue type and are from folk sources or in folk style. The avoidance of the term "duets" in the title reflects the fact that the voices usually alternate, only rarely singing together. Elements of strophic construction are evident but are often superceded by variation or through-composition as the implications of the text demand.

An important contribution to dramatic verity is the use of various voice types as appropriate—alto and tenor for the mother and son in "Edward," soprano and alto for the daughter and mother in "Guter Rat," soprano and tenor to portray the lovers in "So laß uns wandern!" and two sopranos as mother and child in "Walpurgisnacht."

Edward, Op. 75/1

Translated from the Scottish
by Johann Gottfried von Herder (1744–1803)

Dein Schwert, wie ist's von Blut so rot?	Why is your sword so red with blood?
Edward, Edward!	Edward, Edward!
Dein Schwert, wie ist's von Blut so rot,	Why is your sword so red with blood,
Und gehst so traurig her—O!	and you approach so sadly?—O!
"O, ich hab' geschlagen meinen Geier tot,	"O, I have struck my falcon dead,
Mutter, Mutter!	Mother, Mother!
O, ich hab' geschlagen meinen Geier tot,	Oh, I have struck my falcon dead,
Und keinen hab' ich wie er—O!"	and I have no other like him—O!"
Dein's Geiers Blut ist nicht so rot,	Your falcon's blood is not so red,
Edward, Edward!	Edward, Edward!
Dein's Geiers Blut ist nicht so rot,	Your falcon's blood is not so red,
Mein Sohn, bekenn' mir frei—O!	my son, confess to me freely—O!
"O, ich hab' geschlagen mein Rotroß tot,	"Oh, I have struck my roan steed dead,
Mutter, Mutter!	Mother, Mother!
O, ich hab' geschlagen mein Rotroß tot,	Oh, I have struck my roan steed dead,
Und 's war so stolz und treu—O!"	that was so noble and true—O!"
Dein Roß war alt und hast's nicht not,	Your steed was old and you need it not,
Edward, Edward!	Edward, Edward!
Dein Roß war alt und hast's nicht not,	Your steed was old and you need it not,
Dich drückt ein and'rer Schmerz—O!	some other sorrow oppresses you—O!

"O, ich hab' geschlagen meinen
                    Vater tot,
            Mutter, Mutter!
O, ich hab' geschlagen meinen Vater
                    tot,
        Und weh, weh ist mein Herz—O!"

Und was für Buße willst du nun
                    tun?
            Edward, Edward!
Und was für Buße willst du nun tun?
        Mein Sohn, bekenn' mir
                    mehr—O!
"Auf Erden soll mein Fuß nicht
                    ruh'n,
            Mutter, Mutter!
Auf Erden soll mein Fuß nicht ruh'n,
        Will geh'n fern über's Meer—O!"

Und was soll werden dein Hof
                    und Hall?
            Edward, Edward!
Und was soll werden dein Hof
                    und Hall?
        So herrlich sonst und schön—O!
"Ich laß es steh'n, bis es sink' und
                    fall',
            Mutter, Mutter!
Ich laß es steh'n bis es sink' und fall',
        Mag nie es wiederseh'n—O!"

Und was soll werden dein Weib
                    und Kind?
            Edward, Edward!
Und was soll werden dein Weib
                    und Kind?
        Wann du gehst über Meer?—O!
"Die Welt ist groß, laß sie betteln
                    drin,
            Mutter, Mutter!
Die Welt ist groß, laß sie betteln drin,
        Ich seh' sie nimmermehr—O!"

Und was willst du lassen deiner
                    Mutter teu'r?
            Edward, Edward!
Und was willst du lassen deiner Mutter
                    teu'r?
        Mein Sohn, das sage mir—O!

"Oh, I have struck my father
                    dead,
            Mother, Mother!
Oh, I have struck my father dead,

        And sore, sore is my heart—O!"

And now what penance will
                    you do?
            Edward, Edward!
And now what penance will you do?
        My son, confess more to
                    me—O!
"My feet shall not find rest on earth,

            Mother, Mother!
My feet shall not find rest on earth,
        I'll go far across the sea—O!"

And what will become of your house
                    and home?
            Edward, Edward!
And what will become of your house
                    and home,
        once so splendid and fair?—O!
"I'll let it stand 'til it decays and falls,

            Mother, Mother!
I'll let it stand 'til it decays and falls,
        may I never see it again—O!"

And what will become of your wife
                    and child?
            Edward, Edward!
And what will become of your wife
                    and child,
        when you go overseas?—O!
"The world is large, let them beg in it,

            Mother, Mother!
The world is large, let them beg in it,
        I'll never see them again—O!"

And what will you leave your mother
                    dear?
            Edward, Edward!
And what will you leave your mother
                    dear?
        My son, tell me that—O!

"Fluch will ich euch lassen und
      höllisch Feu'r,
   Mutter, Mutter!
Fluch will ich euch lassen und höllisch
         Feu'r,
Denn Ihr, Ihr rietet's mir—O!"

"I'll leave you a curse and the fires of
      hell,
   Mother, Mother!
I'll leave you a curse and the fires of
         hell,
because you, you bade me do
         it—O!"

F minor; common time; *Allegro;* AT.

Approximate duration: 4'10.
Varied (double) strophic.
Composed in 1877; Clara Schumann received a manuscript copy on 13 August.

The first public performance was 17 December 1879 in Vienna at a concert given by Josef Gänsbacher and his students. A private performance by Amalie Joachim and Raimund von Zur Mühlen, who sang from manuscript, took place on 14 November 1878 at Simrock's house in Berlin.

The text is from Herder's *Volkslieder* (Leipzig, 1778–1779), retitled *Stimmen der Völker in Liedern* in 1807. Herder's source was Thomas Percy's *Reliques of Ancient English Poetry* (London, 1765), where the ballad is attributed to "a manuscript copy transmitted from Scotland" and begins:

Quhy dois zour brand sae drop wi' bluid,
      Edward, Edward?
Quhy dois zour brand sae drop wi' bluid?
      And quhy sae sad gang zee, O?
O, I hae killed my hauke sae guid,
      Mither, Mither:
O, I hae killed my hauke sae guid:
      And I had nae mair bot hee, O.

The same verses inspired the first of Brahms's Op. 10 piano ballades in 1854, but there is little, if any, musical resemblance between the two works.

Almost certainly Brahms was familiar with Carl Loewe's melodramatic setting of "Edward," composed in 1818 and published as his Op. 1/1 (Berlin, 1824). Like Loewe, Brahms treats the grisly text in two parts, building to one climax with the son's confession of his father's murder at the end of verse 3 and another, more intense climax with the cursing of the mother at the end of the poem. Also like Loewe's treatment is the importance given by Brahms to the word "O" at the end of each half-stanza of the poem—it becomes one of the most striking features of the setting, although, as

Fuller-Maitland points out, the "O" was doubtless intended as a "meaningless extension of the line, just as 'ah' or 'sir' was often put into the refrain of rustic songs" (*Brahms,* 194).

The rise to the first climax is accomplished primarily through increasing complexity in the accompaniment. Strophe 1 begins with ominous right-hand sixteenths over a throbbing dominant pedal in the bass. The sixteenth notes enclose a skeletal doubling of the mother's melody and a rudimentary harmonization of Edward's response; in the second half the pedal point appears as agitated afterbeats, changing pitch to define the cadences. In the first part of strophe 2 the left hand also participates in the sixteenth-note figure, which is rearranged to produce a four-octave doubling of the melody and an inner pedal; afterbeat basses reappear in the second part but, no longer static, they now constitute the bass line of a new, more active harmonization emphasizing the subdominant. As strophe 3 begins, the doubled sixteenth-note figure becomes the leading voice in a canon with the alto; a constant *crescendo* leads from *pianissimo* to *forte* for the entrance of the tenor, whose melody lies a fourth higher than before and is accompanied by a new martial accompaniment with full chords on the afterbeats. The momentary D♭-major coloration underlines the drama. A repetition of the lamenting "O" in *piano* allows the tension to abate for the start of a new section.

In the second part, rising pitch is the principal tension-increasing device. Each new area of questioning by the mother lies a whole step higher than that preceding. Edward's response in strophe 5 is at the same pitch as that of strophe 4, but in strophe 6 it leaps a third to join in the stepwise climb to B♭ minor for the final strophe.

But much of the electrifying effect of this closing section (like the first) derives from the continually developing, perpetual motion accompaniment with its reharmonizations, its variants, its fluctuating rhythmic complication, and its ever-new figurations. Again the climactic moments feature full chords in the piano. A slight alteration leads back to F minor for the ending and gives the tenor his first obligatory A♭. Once more the despairing "O" is repeated *piano,* and it is left to the turbulent piano postlude to summarize the emotional range of the piece and to confirm the anguish of its characters.

"Edward" was unmistakably a masterpiece, and it attracted more than the usual amount of comment from the three friends whose opinions Brahms customarily sought—Clara Schumann, Theodor Billroth, and Elisabeth von Herzogenberg. On 20 August 1877 Clara wrote from Spinabad to say how much she enjoyed the ballad, which she had received a week earlier:

> The words are horrible, but your setting is wonderful. In spite of the many repetitions of the motif it is always interesting. It recurs in such a variety

of ways in accordance with each change of feeling, and every time it strikes one as new. I cannot tell you how often we have played it together ([Alfred] Volkland [musical director at Basel] and I). Oh, if we only had a couple of singers such as [Heinrich] Vogl and [Marianne] Brandt with us! The piece reminded me of them all the time. You want the ballad back, so I am sending it to you tomorrow morning. I should like to keep it, but do not want to appear ungrateful by abusing your kindness.

The following summer, while Brahms was considering publication of the work, she wrote from Wildbad-Gastein on 16 July 1878:

> "Edward," apart from the fact that it cannot but make a tremendous impression upon anyone who cares for music, is such a masterpiece that you would be sinning against yourself if you did not publish it. If the singers do not sing it, it will be because there are few capable of singing such a work. It can never appeal to a large audience but it will have an enthusiastic one.

Upon his receipt from Brahms of manuscripts of "Edward" and some other "dubious and questionable love stories," Billroth responded from Vienna on 8 November 1877:

> Your "Edward," which up to the present attracts me in almost a magnetic way, will scarcely be something that friend Hans [Eduard Hanslick, noted for his conservative taste] will like. The concept of an orchestra with this mountainous, foggy Scottish atmosphere seems to be the right one. On the other hand, I have thought of a simple form of song, like your "Falkenstein" [Op. 43/4], which today still works the same magic upon me as when [first] heard.

Elisabeth, when returning her copy of "Edward" (which, to Brahms's amusement, she persisted in spelling "Eduard") from Leipzig on 31 January 1878, wrote glowingly:

> Here is your Eduard again. I have taken the liberty of falling more and more hopelessly in love with him. You have no notion what a gorgeous thing it is. . . . Oh for the gift of words to describe this masterpiece! And how natural, how necessary and exactly right it all is! . . . Just as if Eduard's excitement and his mother's must inevitably have had that note from the very beginning, and could have no existence apart from the music. And to think that the poem has lain there so long, a dumb thing, until someone came along, took it to his heart, and gave it to the world again in F minor—his own!
>
> But ours too; for enjoyment is possession.

Guter Rat, Op. 75/2 (Good advice)

Text from Des Knaben Wunderhorn

Ach Mutter, liebe Mutter,
Ach, gebt mir einen Rat!
Es reitet mir alle Frühmorgen
Ein hurtiger Reuter nach.

"Ach Tochter, liebe Tochter!
Den Rat, den geb' ich dir:
Laß du den Reuter fahren,
Bleib' noch ein Jahr bei mir!"

Ach Mutter, liebe Mutter,
Der Rat der ist nicht gut;
Der Reuter, der ist mir lieber
Als alle dein Hab und Gut.

"Ist dir der Reuter lieber
Als alle mein Hab und Gut,
So bind' dein' Kleider zusammen
Und lauf' dem Reuter nach!"

Ach Mutter, liebe Mutter,
Der Kleider hab' ich nicht viel;
Gib mir nur hundert Taler,
So kauf' ich, was ich will.

"Ach Tochter, liebe Tochter,
Der Taler hab' ich nicht viel;
Dein Vater hat alles verrauschet
In Würfel- und Kartenspiel."

Hat mein Vater alles verrauschet
In Würfel- und Kartenspiel,
So sei es Gott geklaget,
Daß ich sein' Tochter bin.

Wär' ich ein Knab' geboren,
Ich wollte ziehn über Feld,
Ich wollte die Trommel rühren
Dem Kaiser wohl um sein Geld.

Oh, Mother, dear Mother,
oh, give me some advice!
A dashing horseman follows me
early each morning.

"Oh, daughter, dear daughter!
The advice that I give you:
let the horseman ride on,
stay with me another year!"

Oh, Mother, dear Mother,
that advice is not good;
the horseman, he is dearer to me
than everything you own.

"If the horseman is dearer to you
then everything I own,
then pack up all your clothes
and run after the horseman!"

Oh, Mother, dear Mother,
I don't have many dresses;
just give me a hundred talers,
so I can buy whatever I want.

"Oh, daughter, dear daughter,
I don't have many talers;
your father lost everything
playing dice and cards."

If my father lost everything
playing dice and cards,
then let it be lamented to God
that I am his daughter.

If I had been born a boy,
I'd march through battlefields,
I'd beat the big drum
for the emperor, indeed, for his money.

E major; $\frac{2}{4}$; *Lebhaft und lustig* (lively and merrily [voices]), *Allegretto giocoso* (piano); SA.

Approximate duration: 1'55.

Varied (double) strophic with elements of ternary form.

Composed in 1877; Theodor Billroth's letter of 11 November 1877 refers to "the duets," of which "I am especially pleased with the 'Rider'!"

A private performance of "Guter Rat" (and "So laß uns wandern!") took place at Billroth's house in Vienna on 29 January 1878; Ottilie Ebner-Hauer, Rosa Girzick, and Filip Forstén sang from manuscript. The first public performance is not documented.

The text is from *Des Knaben Wunderhorn* (Heidelberg, 1806–1808) by Achim von Arnim and Clemens Brentano. Brahms used the poem beginning with verse 7, conscientiously restoring several archaic usages that Brentano and Arnim had changed or modernized. An obvious example is Brahms's archaic "Reuter" for the horseman; in the *Wunderhorn*, the daughter uses "Ritter" (knight), and the mother says "Reiter" (rider).

The setting is in Brahms's sophisticated quasi-folk style, and its light tone and simple textures contrast sharply with the stormy drama and orchestral sonorities of the preceding "Edward." Most of the daughter's strophes (1, 3, 5, and 8) are related by melodic shape, rhythm, or phrase structure as are those of the mother (2, 4, and 6). The mother's opening phrase is an approximate inversion of that of the daughter.

Strophes 1–4 and 8 alternate the tonic and dominant keys. Strophes 5–7 (the apparent B section) digress through G major, E minor, and B minor before reestablishing B major as dominant.

The piano accompaniment's basic pattern of continuous eighths with afterbeat chords often has triplets superimposed. Several passages are noteworthy: the introduction's reversal of the afterbeat pattern; the canterlike rhythm in mm. 7–10 at the first mention of the horseman; the increasingly chromatic sighing figures that accompany the daughter's appeal for money to buy dresses in mm. 47–57; the not-quite-chromatic scale figure that rises *portato* through the mother's revelation of the father's gambling in mm. 62–65, and again staccato through the daughter's rephrasing of it in mm. 69–72; and the delirious, waltzlike final section with its cross-rhythmed postlude.

So laß uns wandern! Op. 75/3 (So let us roam)

Translated from the Bohemian by Joseph Wenzig (1807–1876)

Ach, Mädchen, liebes Mädchen,	Oh maiden, dear maiden,
Wie schwarz dein Auge ist!	how dark your eyes are!
Fast fürcht' ich, es verzaubert	I almost fear they will bewitch me
Mich einst mit arger List.	someday with evil cunning.
"Und wär' mein Auge schwärzer,	"And were my eyes darker,
Um vieles schwärzer noch,	and much darker yet,

Dich, Liebster mein, verzaubern,
Ich tät' es niemals doch."

Die Kräh' auf jener Eiche,
Sieh', wie sie Eicheln pickt!
Wer weiß, wen einst der Himmel
Zum Bräutigam dir schickt!

"Und sprich', wen sollt' er schicken?
Ich gab ja dir mein Wort,
Weißt, unter'm grünen Baume,
Bei uns'rer Hütte dort."

Wohlan, so laß uns wandern,
Du wanderst frisch mit mir;
Ein Kleid von grüner Farbe,
Mein Mädchen, kauf' ich dir.

"Ein Kleid von grüner Farbe,
Das auch nicht gar zu lang:
So kann ich mit dir wandern,
Nichts hindert mich im Gang."

Wir wollen lustig wandern,
Bergüber und talein;
Die großen, freien Wälder
Sind unser Kämmerlein.

my darling, even then
I would never bewitch you."

The crow in that oak tree,
see how it pecks at acorns!
Who knows whom heaven will send you
someday as a bridegroom!

"And tell me, whom should it send?
Indeed, I gave you my word,
you know it, under the green tree
there by our cottage."

Well then, let us roam,
you'll roam eagerly with me;
I'll buy you a
green-colored dress, my girl.

"A green-colored dress
that also is not too long:
so that I can roam with you,
nothing should hinder my movement."

We will roam happily,
over mountains and into valleys;
the vast, open forests
will be our little room.

D major; common time; *Anmutig bewegt und sehr innig* (gracefully moving and very expressive [voices]), *Andante grazioso e molto espressivo* (piano); ST.

Approximate duration: 2′40.

A hybrid form combining elements of ternary form and strophic variation. Strophes 1, 2, and 5–7 are related, as are strophes 3 and 4.

Composed in 1877. This is presumably one of the duets to which Theodor Billroth's letter of 11 December 1877 referred (see the note to "Guter Rat," preceding), since a private performance from manuscript took place in Billroth's home in Vienna on 29 January 1878, with Ottilie Ebner-Hauer and Filip Forstén.

Another private performance from manuscript was sung by Amalie Joachim and Raimund von Zur Mühlen at Simrock's home in Berlin on 14 November 1878. Amalie Joachim and Herr Alvary gave the first public performance on 7 March 1880 in Berlin.

The text is from *Westslawischer Märchenschatz* (Leipzig, 1857).

The setting is notably free of the conflict implied by the opening verses, unfolding amiably in sunny D major with some poignant nods at E minor. The central section leans toward G major with turns to F♯ minor in stanza 3 and, affectingly, F major in stanza 4. The dialogue of stanzas 1–5 out of the way, the two voices join in happy agreement for stanzas 6 and 7. Their music begins with what would have been the final phrase of the principal strophe, progresses through a short development emphasizing the sub-dominant to a *fermata* on the dominant, and concludes with an expansive variant of the main strophe.

The vocal melody begins with a characteristic broken chord without a tonic; two similar figures in the introduction reach D and A, framing and preparing the tenor's top F♯. The right hand of the accompaniment is in the treble for strophe 1 but in the tenor range for strophe 2, clearing the registers of the tenor and soprano voice respectively. Four-measure phrases are the norm, but the final phrase of strophes 1 and 7 is stretched to five measures.

Both Elisabeth von Herzogenberg and Clara Schumann responded with less than their usual enthusiasm when given a prepublication look at "So laß uns wandern!" Elisabeth wrote on 16 January 1878:

> I am studying the D major duet with W——, the tenor, and take immense pains to get it nice; but W—— can't manage the B♭-E-A-D at the end in the chamber scene [at "unser Kämmerlein," m. 67], which makes singing together very difficult.

In June 1878 Brahms wrote to Clara from Pörtschach:

> I also send you some duets which I intend to publish with "Edward." Please write and say what you think of them.

A few weeks later she replied from Wildbad-Gastein (9 July 1878):

> I will pick up courage for one thing and that is to beg you not to print . . . the D major duet ["So laß uns wandern!"], for I should put [it] down to anyone rather than to you.

Walpurgisnacht, Op. 75/4 (Walpurgis night)
Text by Willibald Alexis
(pseudonym of Wilhelm Häring, 1798–1871)

Lieb' Mutter, heut' Nacht heulte Regen
und Wind.
—"Ist heute der erste Mai, liebes
Kind!"

Dear Mother, this night the rain and
wind howled.
—"Today is the first of May, dear
child!"

Lieb' Mutter, es donnerte auf dem
　　Brocken oben.
—"Lieb' Kind, es waren die Hexen
　　droben."

Liebe Mutter, ich möcht' keine Hexen
　　sehn.
—"Liebes Kind, es ist wohl schon oft
　　geschehn."

Liebe Mutter, ob im Dorf wohl Hexen
　　sind?
—"Sie sind dir wohl näher, mein liebes
　　Kind."

Ach, Mutter, worauf fliegen die Hexen
　　zum Berg?
—"Auf Nebel, auf Rauch, auf
　　loderndem Werg."

Ach, Mutter, was reiten die Hexen
　　beim Spiel?
—"Sie reiten, sie reiten den
　　Besenstiel."

Ach, Mutter, was fegten im Dorfe die
　　Besen!
—"Es sind auch viel Hexen auf'm
　　Berge gewesen."

Ach, Mutter, was hat es im Schornstein
　　gekracht!
—"Es flog auch wohl Eine hinaus über
　　Nacht."

Ach, Mutter, dein Besen war die Nacht
　　nicht zu Haus!
—"Lieb's Kind, so war er zum Brocken
　　hinaus."

Ach, Mutter, dein Bett war leer in der
　　Nacht!
—"Deine Mutter hat oben auf dem
　　Blocksberg gewacht."

Dear Mother, it thundered up on the
　　Brocken.
—"Dear child, there were witches up
　　there."

Dear Mother, I don't want to see any
　　witches.
—"Dear child, it has probably already
　　happened often."

Dear Mother, are there really witches in
　　the village?
—"They are even closer to you, my
　　dear child."

Oh, Mother, on what do witches fly to
　　the mountain?
—"On mist, on smoke, on
　　burning tow."

Oh, Mother, what do witches ride when
　　they're playing?
—"They ride, they ride on
　　broomsticks."

Oh, Mother, how the brooms swept in
　　the village!
—"There were also many witches on
　　the mountain."

Oh, Mother, such a crash there was in
　　the chimney!
—"One may indeed have flown out
　　during the night."

Oh, Mother, your broom was not in the
　　house last night!
—"Dear child, then it was out on the
　　Brocken."

Oh, Mother, your bed was empty
　　during the night!
—"Your mother was on watch up on
　　the Blocksberg."

A minor; $\frac{2}{4}$ (voices), $\frac{6}{8}$ (piano); *Presto;* S.I, S.II.

Approximate duration: 1′25.

Through-composed, with elements of strophic variation.

Composed in February 1878 in Vienna.

The first performance took place on 14 February 1881 in Vienna at a *Liederabend* of Gustav Walter with Sophie Hanslick.

The text was first printed in Alexis's essay "Über Balladenpoesie" in *Hermes, oder kritisches Jahrbuch der Literatur XXI* (1824); Brahms used a revision published later in the poet's *Balladen* (Berlin, 1836). As in the case of "Edward," there was an earlier setting of "Walpurgisnacht" by Carl Loewe, published in 1824 and based on, though somewhat differing from, the earlier version of the poem.

Walpurgis Night, named for St. Walburga (d. A.D. 777), an English saint whose feast day falls on May Day, is the evening of 30 April (May Day eve) when, as was widely held—particularly during medieval and Renaissance times—witches celebrate a sabbath. Still today there are places where bonfires are kept burning all night to repel the evil spirits. The Brocken (also known as the Blocksberg) is the highest point in the Harz Mountains and was believed to be a site for the witches' gathering.

As Clara Schumann noted in her letter of 9 July 1878, the setting is "a worthy companion to the ballad of 'Edward'"; in both, each in a series of exchanges reveals another layer of a dreadful truth while the music increases inexorably in dramatic tension toward a nearly unbearable climax.

The piano introduction is based on a chromatic rhythmic motive that first suggests fear; later in the piece, dread; and finally, the embodiment of satanic evil. It underlies the child's part of exchanges 1 through 6 and the mother's responses thereafter, and it constitutes the building material for the postlude.

The child is given two melodic shapes: the first (mm. 6–10) rises overall but features stepwise descending thirds and, with its variants, it appears in the first five exchanges; the second (mm. 46–50) has two similar halves with a falling fifth between and, with its variants, serves the child for the remainder of the piece.

The mother's words are set to three basic shapes. The first (mm. 10–14) falls overall, first stepwise and then into a cadence pattern; it appears in exchanges 1–4, and the piano bass doubles its initial scalar third three octaves below. The second, which appears in exchanges 5 and 6, also falls through an octave, but it resembles a bass line more than a melody—the piano bass in fact doubles each downbeat and the last three notes—and is accompanied by a piano melody resembling the first of the child. The third appears in exchanges 7–9 and is an inversion of the child's second shape with another fifth (now rising) appended at the end; it is accompanied in the piano by its own original (the child's) form; the mother's final line of text is first sung to a variant that substitutes a fourth for the interior and ending fifth and is then repeated to an expanded version of the child's second melody itself.

At the outset, there seems to be a straightforward unfolding of question-and-answer units (musically, if not always linguistically). The four-measure question rises in pitch to end on a weak cadence that requires an answer, which falls in pitch, usually to a cadence on the dominant, inviting an ensuing question. The regularity is superficially reassuring, and mother and child address each other as "dear." But not all is what it seems, or what it ought to be.

The child initiates the conversation but skirts the real question— "Mother, are you a witch?" In fact, only three questions are asked, none of them bearing directly on the mother's activities. It seems clear that the child suspects the truth but fears hearing its confirmation, hoping desperately for denial instead.

The mother, on the other hand, soon wrests control of the dialogue from the child, always providing more information than is requested—she uses the child's opening remarks about the weather to turn to the subject of witches—to the growing horror of the child. Possessed by demonic forces, the mother is increasingly driven to reveal her secret.

Suddenly in exchange 5 the mother-child relationship begins to disintegrate, and the mother starts to become a witch before our (and the child's) eyes. The endearing "lieb' Mutter" and "liebes Kind" are cast aside, hysteria drives the child's query a third higher than before, and the comfortable environment of A minor and related keys is abandoned for the unanchored chromaticism of the supernatural.

From the C basis of exchange 5, each eight-measure group rises a half step to the E♭ of exchange 8. The ninth moves on through E to F to F♯; the tenth, from G through G♯ (made dominant by the addition of a bass E) to an electrifying silence, the first since the hectic dialogue began.

When the no-longer-mother reenters in A minor, her transformation is complete, and she has absorbed the child's identity in the process. Her entrance, late, with phrases of five and six measures destroys the four-measure convention. Those phrases in themselves constitute a question-and-answer segment, obliterating the child's function. Further, she has bested the child's vocal range at both extremes and appropriated the child's melody as her own, having gradually taken possession of it since the crucial fifth exchange.

(Much of the preceding is indebted to Raphael Atlas's imaginative, detailed analysis ["Text and Musical Gesture," 248–58].)

In response to the receipt of a manuscript copy of "Walpurgisnacht," Elisabeth von Herzogenberg wrote at some length and with approbation on 1 March 1878 from her home in Leipzig:

> You know the delight with which we in Humboldtstrasse hail every shaving from your workshop; how much greater our delight over this thrilling witch-duet, which is one unbroken flow of inspiration. . . . The words seem

to me quite blood-curdling, and I was furious with an enlightened professor to whom I lent the poem the other day. It only struck him as intensely ludicrous, poor fellow! *He* was not brought up on Grimm's fairy tales. I am glad to say the duet sends cold shudders down my back every time I play it, although I know quite well by now that the mother has flown up the chimney. I am going to practice it with the youngest Röntgen girl. Her innocent childish soprano is the very thing for the witch's daughter, and I intend to distinguish myself as the witch. And how delightful it all is again! The whole situation is so clear from the very opening, and I like the way the bass doubles the voice in "Ist heute der erste Mai, liebes Kind," and, farther on, the introduction of the frightened daughter's motif into the accompaniment to the mother's replies (let anyone with a desire to shudder and shake come and listen), which makes that part as much a duet as if the daughter's voice were heard. Of course the answer is the question inverted—that one would expect! And how it works up to a climax at the end—there is a family resemblance to "Edward" there!

Five Romances and Songs for One or Two Voices

OPUS 84

Romanzen und Lieder für eine oder zwei Stimmen mit Begleitung des Pianoforte von Johannes Brahms (Romances and songs for one or two voices with piano accompaniment by Johannes Brahms), Op. 84. Published in July 1882 by N. Simrock in Berlin; publication number 8298; German text only.

Although there is no dedication, Max Kalbeck conjectured that these five songs were intended for Amalie Joachim, citing her dramatic skill, her varied vocal color, and her ability to "alternate between soprano and alto, both of which are joined in her ample mezzo-soprano" (*Johannes Brahms,* III₂, 338–39). They can be (and usually are) performed by a single versatile singer, but their dialogue format makes them effective also as duets; duet performance is actually preferable for the fifth, "Spannung," because of its length, its emotional range, and the optional second voice part in the last strophe.

Elisabeth von Herzogenberg found the Op. 84 songs particularly delightful, and she wrote to Brahms on 24 July 1882:

> The little ones for one or two voices, *ad libitum,* are the winningest little rogues. How innocent they are! It is like looking into the faces of children—well-brought-up children, such as, say, Schubert's or Beethoven's might be.

Sommerabend, Op. 84/1 (Summer evening)

Text by Hans Schmidt (1856–?)

Geh' schlafen, Tochter, schlafen!
Schon fällt der Tau auf's Gras,
Und wen die Tropfen trafen,
Weint bald die Augen naß!

"Laß weinen, Mutter, weinen!

Das Mondlicht leuchtet hell,
Und wem die Strahlen scheinen,
Dem trocknen Tränen schnell!"

Geh' schlafen, Tochter, schlafen!
Schon ruft der Kauz im Wald,
Und wen die Töne trafen,
Muß mit ihm klagen bald!

"Laß klagen, Mutter, klagen!

Die Nachtigall singt hell,
Und wem die Lieder schlagen,
Dem schwindet Trauer schnell!"

Go to sleep, daughter, to sleep!
Already the dew is falling on the grass,
and whomever the drops touch
will soon cry his eyes wet!

"Forget the crying, Mother, the crying!

The moonlight is shining brightly,
and whomever the beams shine upon,
for him tears will dry quickly!"

Go to sleep, daughter, to sleep!
Already the owl is hooting in the forest,
and whomever the sounds reach
must soon lament with it!

"Forget the lamenting, Mother, the lamenting!

The nightingale is singing clearly,
and whomever the songs fall upon,
for him grief disappears quickly!"

D minor/major; $\frac{2}{4}$; *Andante con moto;* daughter, mother [SA].

Approximate duration: 1′40.

(Double) strophic. Except for slight differences in the harmonization, the mother's two verses are set to the same music in minor, and the daughter's two are set alike to different music in the major; the two strophes are related by rhythm and phrase structure.

Probably composed during summer 1881 at Preßbaum bei Wien—in a letter from that summer Brahms thanks Schmidt effusively for his having sent a copy of *Gedichte und Übersetzungen* (Offenbach am Main, no date), from which the text is taken.

Ida Seelig gave the first public performance on 21 May 1895 in Hamburg, accompanied by Julius Spengel.

The two characters are contrasted not only by mode but by tessitura, accompaniment style (though sustained afterbeats are the norm), and the construction of their melodies. The mother's line is mostly stepwise with many uneasy dissonances, while the daughter's has more skips and is almost entirely consonant. The sighing afterbeats in the accompaniment suggest the weeping and lamenting of the text; the cheerful rising triplets against eighths in the daughter's music offer momentary reassurance.

Elisabeth von Herzogenberg wrote from Graz on 24 July 1882:

> I can hardly imagine anything prettier or daintier than the lines of the mother's melody in "Sommerabend," and the repetition of that one line of the words. How ingeniously that part finishes, too! I delight in every little stroke, as if it were a fine old engraving—by [C. W.] Dietrich, say, in whose work art and strong natural emotion are as indistinguishably blended.

Der Kranz, Op. 84/2 (The garland)

Text by Hans Schmidt (1856–?)

Mutter, hilf mir armen Tochter,	Mother, help me, your poor daughter;
Sieh' nur, was ein Knabe tat;	just see what some boy did:
Einen Kranz von Rosen flocht er,	he braided a garland of roses,
Den er mich zu tragen bat!	which he begged me to wear!
"Ei, sei deshalb unerschrocken,	"Oho, don't be alarmed by that,
Helfen läßt sich dir gewiß!	there is certainly a way to help you!
Nimm den Kranz nur aus den Locken,	Just take the garland out of your hair,
Und den Knaben, den vergiß."	and as for the boy, forget him."
Dornen hat der Kranz, o Mutter,	The garland has thorns, O Mother,
Und die halten fest das Haar!	and they hold my hair fast!
Worte sprach der Knabe, Mutter,	The boy said some things, Mother,
An die denk' ich immerdar!	that I think about constantly!

G minor/major; $\frac{6}{8}$; *Lebhaft* (lively [voices]), *Allegro grazioso* (piano); daughter, mother [SA].

Approximate duration: 1'35.

Through-composed, though the last verse begins like the first.

Probably composed during summer 1881 at Preßbaum bei Wien.

Amalie Joachim gave the first performance on 17 February 1884 in Berlin.

The text is from *Gedichte und Übersetzungen* (Offenbach am Main, no date).

The two characters are differentiated by vocal range, tessitura, and the character of the music assigned to each.

The emotional distress resulting from the daughter's dilemma is suggested by the several appoggiaturas in her melody and by the tremulous accompaniment. The garland obviously has great significance: the phrase in which she first mentions it is expanded to three measures and modulates to the relative major, in which key her quiet reiteration that the boy has asked her to wear it is also stretched to three measures.

The mother's more triadic music, on the other hand, reflects greater strength, but she too is troubled by the garland—her reference to it borrows the daughter's uneasy melody and quavery accompaniment.

The daughter begins her response to the same music as before, but her attraction to the boy is too strong. A change to the major mode, *animato* and *forte,* and soaring phrases in the higher register bring the piece to a decisive, impassioned conclusion.

In den Beeren, Op. 84/3 (In the berry patch)

Text by Hans Schmidt (1856–?)

Singe, Mädchen, hell und klar,	Sing, sweet girl, bright and clear,
Sing' aus voller Kehle,	sing at the top of your lungs,
Daß uns nicht die Spatzenschar	so that the flock of sparrows doesn't
Alle Beeren stehle!	steal all our berries.
"Mutter, mag auch weit der Spatz	"Mother, though the sparrow may flee
Fliehn vor meinem Singen,	far to escape my singing,
Fürcht' ich doch, es wird den Schatz	still I fear it will bring
Um so näher bringen."	my sweetheart all the nearer."
Freilich, für so dreisten Gauch	By all means, for so brazen a cuckoo
Braucht es einer Scheuche,	a scarecrow is needed;
Warte nur, ich komme auch	just wait, I'll come into
In die Beerensträuche!	the berry bushes too!
"Mutter! nein, das hat nicht Not!	"No, Mother, that's not necessary:
Beeren, schau, sind teuer,	look, berries are expensive,
Doch der Küsse, reif und rot,	but nowadays there are plenty
Gibt es viele heuer!"	of kisses, ripe and red!"

E♭ major; ²⁄₄; *Sehr lebhaft* (very lively); mother, daughter [S.I, S.II].

Approximate duration: 1′30.

(Double) strophic; the mother's two verses are set to similar music as are, with somewhat more variation, the two of the daughter.

Probably composed during summer 1881 at Preßbaum bei Wien. The first performance is not documented.

The text is from *Gedichte und Übersetzungen* (Offenbach am Main, no date).

Brahms distinguishes the daughter's music from that of the mother not by tessitura but rather by an enharmonic shift to the lowered submediant with added chromaticism and dissonance. Particularly noteworthy are lines 3 and 4 of the daughter's strophes, where the accompaniment in flowing eighths accomplishes the return to the tonic Eb: in strophe 2, each line occupies four measures, and the repetition of line 4 is expanded to five; but in strophe 4, line 3 is also repeated to a total of eight measures, and the repetition of line 4 is stretched to six. The prolongation of the high G in the final phrase and the return of the music of the introduction as postlude combine to impart a satisfying sense of finality.

In her letter of 24 July 1882 from Graz, Elisabeth von Herzogenberg remarked of "In den Beeren":

Perhaps the "Beerenlied" is even more lovable [than "Sommerabend"], in the gay insouciance of its modulation to Eb minor (that chameleon-like key with its D#, so perplexing at the first reading!), and the calm way in which it sidles into B major. I also take some pleasure in the delicate eighth-note accompaniment at the first mention of the "sweetheart," which is so charmingly extended, the second time, to suit the "ripe red kisses," and the sudden and very convincing return to luminous Eb major. Ah yes, the privileged master-hand can carry us at full speed, as unconscious of our actual movements as a beautiful deer in flight; whereas the less supple runner makes us pant and puff in a piteous way.

Vergebliches Ständchen, Op. 84/4 (Unsuccessful serenade)

Text by Anton Wilhelm Florentin von Zuccalmaglio (1803–1869)
Based on a Folk Song from the Lower Rhine

Guten Abend, mein Schatz,	Good evening, my treasure,
Guten Abend, mein Kind!	good evening, my child!
Ich komm' aus Lieb' zu dir,	I come to you out of love;
Ach, mach' mir auf die Tür!	ah, open the door for me,
Mach' mir auf die Tür!	open the door for me!
"Meine Tür ist verschlossen,	"My door is locked,
Ich laß dich nicht ein;	I'll not let you in;
Mutter die rät' mir klug,	Mother advises me wisely;

Wär'st du herein mit Fug,
Wär's mit mir vorbei!"

  So kalt ist die Nacht,
So eisig der Wind,
Daß mir das Herz erfriert,
Mein' Lieb' erlöschen wird;
Öffne mir, mein Kind!

  "Löschet dein' Lieb',
Laß sie löschen nur!
Löschet sie immerzu,
Geh' heim zu Bett zur Ruh',
Gute Nacht, mein Knab'!"

if I permitted you inside,
it would be all over for me!

  So cold is the night,
so icy the wind,
that my heart is freezing;
my love will expire—
open for me, my child!

  "If your love expires,
just let it go out!
If it keeps expiring,
go home to bed to sleep;
good night, my boy!"

  A major; ¾; *Lebhaft und gut gelaunt* (lively and good-humored); female, male [ST].

  Approximate duration: 1′45.
  Strophic with varied accompaniment.
  Probably composed during the summers 1877–1879 in Pörtschach.
  The first performance was on 23 February 1883 in Vienna's Saal Bösendorfer at a *Liederabend* by Gustav Walter with Brahms at the piano.
  The text is from the Kretzschmer-Zuccalmaglio *Deutsche Volkslieder mit ihren Original-Weisen* (Berlin, 1838–1840). It is not an authentic folk song from the Lower Rhine as Brahms presumed but is instead an almost entirely original reworking by Zuccalmaglio of the content of an old folk song. But it is a masterly adaptation, and the setting is one of Brahms's most beloved songs. The composer himself, usually so reticent about his own works, was especially pleased with it; Kalbeck reports that, in response to the critic Eduard Hanslick's singling the song out for praise, Brahms wrote, "It was really something special for me and I am in a particularly good humor about it. . . . For this one song I would sacrifice all the others" (*Johannes Brahms*, III₂, 337).
  The song's breezy charm results from its lack of harmonic complexity, the many reiterations of text, its repetitive rhythms, and above all, the extraordinary economy of its melodic construction.
  The poignancy of the lover's pleading in strophe 3 is heightened by a change to the minor mode and by the interplay between the raised and lowered fourth scale step. A countermelody in running eighth notes evokes the chill wind of the text.
  But the major mode returns with the last phrase, and the interlude's

cross-accents usher in a brighter character for the final strophe. Merrily the girl dismisses the boy's suit to a dancing accompaniment of eighth notes. A *sforzando* chord in the postlude suggests the slamming of the door in his face, but the prevailing lightheartedness undermines the finality of the gesture.

Spannung, Op. 84/5 (Tension)

Folk Song from the Lower Rhine [?]

Gut'n Abend, gut'n Abend, mein
    tausiger Schatz,
Ich sag' dir guten Abend;
Komm' du zu mir, ich komme zu dir,
Du sollst mir Antwort geben, mein
    Engel!

Good evening, good evening, my
    precious treasure,
I bid you good evening;
come to me, I'll come to you;
you must give me an answer, my angel!

Ich kommen zu dir, du kommen
    zu mir?
Das wär' mir gar keine Ehre;
Du gehst von mir zu andern Jung-
    frau'n,
Das hab' ich wohl vernommen, mein
    Engel!

I come to you, you come to me?

That would be no honor at all for me.
You go from me to other girls,

I have that on good authority, my
    angel!

Ach nein, mein Schatz, und glaub' es
    nur nicht,
Was falsche Zungen reden,
Es geben so viele gottlosige Leut',
Die dir und mir nichts gönnen, mein
    Engel!

Oh, no, my darling, and just don't
    believe it,
what false tongues say;
there are so many godless people,
who envy you and me everything, my
    angel!

Und gibt es so viele gottlosige
    Leut',
Die dir und mir nichts gönnen,
So solltest du selber bewahren die
    Treu'
Und machen zu Schanden ihr Reden,
    mein Engel!

And if there are so many godless
    people,
who envy you and me everything,
then you yourself should be faithful

and discredit their gossip, my angel!

Leb' wohl, mein Schatz, ich hör' es
    wohl,
Du hast einen anderen lieber,
So will ich meiner Wege gehn,
Gott möge dich wohl behüten, mein
    Engel!

Farewell, my darling, I hear it
    clearly—
you prefer another man,
so I will go my own way;
may God guard you well, my angel!

Ach nein, ich hab' kein' anderen
    lieb,

Oh, no, I don't love anyone else;

Ich glaub' nicht gottlosigen Leuten,	I don't believe godless people;
Komm' du zu mir, ich komme zu dir,	come to me, I'll come to you;
Wir bleiben uns beide getreue, mein	we'll both be faithful to each other, my
Engel!	angel!

A minor/major; $\frac{3}{8}$; *Bewegt und heimlich* (animatedly and secretively); female, male [ST].

Approximate duration: 3′10.

Varied strophic; A A B B A′ A″. Stanzas 1 and 2 are set to the same music, as are stanzas 3 and 4, the two settings being related by their phrase structure and some rhythmic correspondences. Stanza 5 has the same melody as 1 and 2 but a different accompaniment, and stanza 6 is an expanded variation of the same music in the major.

Probably composed during the summers 1877–1879 in Pörtschach.

The first performance was sung as a duet by Ida Huber-Petzold and Adolf Weber in Basel on 23 January 1883.

The text is from the Kretzschmer-Zuccalmaglio collection *Deutsche Volkslieder mit ihren Original-Weisen* (Berlin, 1838–1840). Brahms had already made an arrangement of the supposed folk song that would be published in 1894 as no. 4 of the forty-nine *Deutsche Volkslieder*, but it is probable that the text, and virtually certain that the melody, had been subjected to Zuccalmaglio's usual tampering. In the *Deutsche Volkslieder* version, the second verse retains Zuccalmaglio's fourth line, "Das kann ich an dir wohl spüren" (I can tell it by looking at you); for the Op. 84 setting, Brahms changed the line to the less accusing "Das hab' ich wohl vernommen" (I have that on good authority). The third verse has "und glaub' es mir nicht" (don't believe it of me) in the *Volkslieder* but "und glaub' es nur nicht" (just don't believe it) in Op. 84.

The setting has the same meter and phrase structure as the folk song arrangement, including the expansion of the last phrase to five measures, and both have a section with a contrasting accompaniment in flowing sixteenth notes. But the insertion of secondary material, the changing character, the rhythmic diversity of the accompaniment, the melodic use of diminished and augmented intervals, and especially the developmental concluding section with its optional harmonizing line, all combine to position the setting nearer to dramatic art song than to authentic folk song style. The contrapuntal interplay between the voice(s) and piano in the last strophe is particularly striking.

In a letter to Brahms of 24 July 1882 from Graz, Elisabeth von Herzogenberg wrote:

> "Spannung" I find strangely touching. "Du sollst mir Antwort geben, mein
> Engel" is so urgent, so sweetly persuasive. The words are so beautiful there,
> and the A major at the close—and the fond union of the voices—is so
> exactly after my own heart; indeed, it goes straight to my heart. And so as
> usual I may close by thanking you sincerely, dear friend, for is it not the
> things which appeal to the heart that make life worth living?

Four Quartets

OPUS 92

Quartette für Sopran, Alt, Tenor und Bass mit Pianoforte von Johannes Brahms
(Quartets for soprano, alto, tenor, and bass with piano by Johannes
Brahms), Op. 92. Score and parts published in December 1884 by N. Simrock in Berlin; publication numbers 8477 (score) and 8478 (parts); in German only.

A distinctive nocturnal, occasionally elegiac, aura pervades all four
quartets. They are marked by ravishing harmonies, discreet (though frequent) use of counterpoint, and imaginative exploitation of color, particularly in the piano writing.

O schöne Nacht! Op. 92/1 (O lovely night!)

Translated from the Hungarian
by Georg Friedrich Daumer (1800–1875)

O schöne Nacht!	O lovely night!
Am Himmel märchenhaft	In the heavens, fairy-tale-like,
Erglänzt der Mond in seiner ganzen Pracht;	the moon shines in all its splendor;
Um ihn der kleinen Sterne liebliche Genossenschaft.	around it, a charming company of little stars.
Es schimmert hell der Tau	The dew glitters brightly
Am grünen Halm; mit Macht	on the green grain; the nightingale

Im Fliederbusche schlägt die Nachtigall;	is singing loudly in the lilac bush;
Der Knabe schleicht zu seiner Liebsten sacht—	the youth creeps softly to his beloved—
O schöne Nacht!	O lovely night!

E major; $\frac{3}{4}$; *Andante con moto;* SATB.

Approximate duration: 3'00.
A B A B' C A'.

Though not published until 1884, probably composed during summer 1877 in Pörtschach and Lichtenthal (near Baden-Baden). Manuscript copies were sent to Elisabeth von Herzogenberg on 12 December 1877 and to Theodor Billroth a bit earlier.

The published version was first performed on 28 January 1885 in Krefeld for the fiftieth anniversary celebration of the Krefeld Singverein. A private performance of the early version took place in Billroth's Vienna home on 29 January 1878, with which date he inscribed his copy.

There is some amusing correspondence relating to the manuscript that was prepared specifically for the Herzogenbergs. In her response of 5 May 1877 to Brahms's customary request for comment on a group of songs to be published as Opp. 69–71, Elisabeth had written:

> Since you insist on hearing what we did not like, I will tell you . . . I don't like ["Tambourliedchen," Op. 69/5] or "Willst du, daß ich geh'" [Op. 71/4]. Particularly the latter fails to appeal to me; the words alone are enough. That kind of reproof is only possible in *Volkston* [(folkloric)] style. . . . this one has an unpleasant ring.

When Brahms sent her "O schöne Nacht" on 12 December, his accompanying letter remarked:

> I will not insult your intelligence by offering to explain the little jest I am sending.

After the passage "Der Knabe schleicht zu seiner Liebsten sacht" (the boy steals softly to his beloved), there is a blank space in the score, in which Brahms had written:

> Stop, Johannes my son, what's this? These matters are only to be treated in *Volkston* style; you have forgotten *again*. Only a peasant may ask whether

he is to stay or go, and you are no peasant, alas! Don't offend that fair
head with its glory of gold, but have done! Repeat simply [here the song
continues] "O schöne Nacht!"

The "jest" was a double one; there is not only a reference to Elisabeth's
objection to "Willst du, daß ich geh'?" but Brahms had also borrowed a
theme from her husband, Heinrich.

On 16 December 1877 Heinrich wrote to Brahms:

> Would it not have been better to fill this serious gap with something nice
> and noncommittal than to exercise your fatal memory for certain conver-
> sations?
>
> I am copying out this exquisite song, and want to have it sung here,
> so please send what is missing.
>
> The youth steals along a familiar path to his beloved, but what matter,
> if he does it melodiously?

Elisabeth added a postscript:

> I have to thank you for the manuscript, which would have pleased me
> better without its strong flavor of sarcasm aimed at my poor feminine
> scruples. You think me prudish, and it is useless to defend myself, al-
> though nothing could be more unjust. If you only knew how many lances
> I have broken for your Daumer songs [Op. 57], even the much-abused
> "Unbewegte laue Luft" [Op. 57/8].
>
> But one gets hardened to ingratitude. It is just the way in which the
> question is put—May he stay?—that makes all the difference, and Lemcke
> is not, to my mind, the man to put it. Now this E-major piece might say or
> ask what it would; it is so beautiful, one would put up with anything. What
> a distressingly good memory you have!

The serene, sonorous arpeggios and glistening treble afterbeats of the
piano's opening conjure up images of warm summer evenings and star-
studded skies. (Both the Herzogenberg and Billroth manuscripts bear the
title "Notturno.") The changing-tone figure in the bass voice in m. 5, imitated by the piano's bass in m. 7 and treble in m. 8 (and freely by the
soprano and tenor voices in m. 6), barely sets the piece in motion. The
noble melody that begins in m. 12, with its slow harmonic rhythm, portrays
the regal moon; the quicker movement in both piano and voice of the
phrase that follows (beginning in m. 20) depicts the "company of little
stars."

Much of the distinctive atmosphere of the piece derives from the un-
usually wide spacings and colorful figurations in the piano writing. Note,
for example, the treble "glittering dew" in mm. 37–39 and the ecstatic war-
bling of the nightingale that begins in m. 41.

The exquisite passage in C major, where the youth steals to his beloved,
has often been singled out (beginning with Heinrich Herzogenberg's let-

ter, cited above). Noteworthy features include the exchange of melodies between voices and piano when the passage is repeated; the apparent broadening to two measures of $\frac{4}{4}$ at the reiterated "sacht, sacht"; the piano bass's canonic imitation in mm. 56–58 of the piano melody immediately preceding; and the effortless change of harmonic color that brings the return of the tonic key at m. 63.

The left-hand figuration in the piano continues to hint at duple meter during the expanded return of the opening material, and it joins the voices in four measures of hemiola to approach the nearly motionless final cadence. Keyboard-spanning arpeggiations at the close recall the initial piano sonorities.

Spätherbst, Op. 92/2 (Late autumn)

Text by Hermann Allmers (1821–1902)

Der graue Nebel tropft so still	The grey mist drops down so quietly
Herab auf Feld und Wald und Heide,	on fields and woods and moors,
Als ob der Himmel weinen will	as if heaven were moved to weep
In übergroßem Leide.	in overwhelming grief.
Die Blumen wollen nicht mehr blühn,	The flowers will no longer bloom,
Die Vöglein schweigen in den Hainen,	the little birds are silent in the groves,
Es starb sogar das letzte Grün,	even the last bit of greenery has died;
Da mag er auch wohl weinen.	indeed, heaven may well be weeping.

E minor; $\frac{3}{4}$; *Andante;* SATB.

Approximate duration: 1′40.

Varied strophic; A A′.

Probably composed during summer 1884, although the details of composition are unclear. A letter from Billroth to Brahms dated 6 August 1884 refers to the receipt of various manuscripts, including "five [*sic*] quartets with piano accompaniment" which "make up a nice volume," specifically mentioning "O schöne Nacht," "Spätherbst," "Abendlied," and "the verse of Goethe." But the letter also discusses "Tafellied," a work for six-part mixed chorus with piano that was to be published in January 1885 as Op. 93b; it seems likely that Billroth's reference to "five quartets" was mere carelessness.

"Spätherbst" was first performed (together with "O schöne Nacht," Op.

92/1, and the first performance of "Warum?" Op. 92/4) on 4 February 1889 in Frankfurt am Main.

The text is from Allmers's *Dichtungen* (Bremen, 1860).

Over a pizzicato bass, the three lower voices begin as though to provide a harmonic foundation for a predominant soprano melody, but soon all are drawn into the flowing contrapuntal texture. The most memorable motive is that sung by the soprano in m. 4 and imitated immediately by the alto in m. 5. Another statement and imitation occur in mm. 7 and 8, and finally at "übergroßem Leide," the climax of the strophe, it appears successively in soprano, alto, and bass in mm. 12–15. Its grieving triplets eloquently set the mournful tone of the piece, and indeed, toward the end that motive and related materials set the word "weinen" over and over.

In the second strophe, the introductory two measures for the lower voices are compressed into two beats, and the accompaniment is given legato right-hand chords to replace the earlier staccato suggestions of falling droplets of mist. The tenor and bass parts differ considerably from those of the first strophe; the tenor in particular is more florid and now duets with the soprano as well as the alto in the triplet motive. The end of the strophe is extended by text repetition to allow a touching change to the tonic major and a long trailing off at "auch wohl weinen." With its hemiola broadening and fermata, the piano extends the gradual decline into the postlude.

Abendlied, Op. 92/3 (Evening song)

Text by Friedrich Hebbel (1813–1863)

Friedlich bekämpfen	Peacefully night and day
Nacht sich und Tag;	oppose each other;
Wie das zu dämpfen,	how that can assuage,
Wie das zu lösen vermag.	how it can dispel.
Der mich bedrückte,	That which oppressed me,
Schläfst du schon, Schmerz?	are you already asleep, suffering?
Was mich beglückte,	That which gladdened me,
Sage, was war's doch, mein Herz?	tell me, my heart, what was it then?
Freude wie Kummer,	Both joy and sorrow
Fühl' ich, zerrann,	melted away, I feel,
Aber den Schlummer	but they gently
Führten sie leise heran.	ushered in slumber.
Und im Entschweben,	And in their vanishing,
Immer empor,	ever aloft,
Kommt mir das Leben	life to me seems
Ganz wie ein Schlummerlied vor.	just like a lullaby.

F major; common time; *Andante;* SATB.

Approximate duration: 2′30.

A hybrid form combining elements of through-composition and strophic variation; two large sections that begin alike but proceed differently.

Presumably composed during summer 1884, although the details are unclear. A letter of 6 August 1884 from Billroth to Brahms acknowledges the receipt of several manuscripts, including "quartets with piano accompaniment," among them "Abendlied."

The first performance is not documented.

Brahms owned Hebbel's *Sämmtliche Werke* (Hamburg, 1865–1867). The poem was originally entitled "Abendgefühl" (Evening sentiment).

Each half of the setting begins with homophonic vocal writing over a rather prosaic accompaniment figure, which is announced in the introduction and consists of a two-measure ostinato-like bass—an arpeggio upward and a cadence formula downward—with afterbeat chords in the right hand. The first such section sets stanza 1 and veers to D major (the submediant) in its second phrase; the other sets stanza 3 and part of stanza 4, and its analogous harmonic excursion is to D♭ major (the lowered submediant).

In breathtaking contrast, stanza 2 (mm. 15–28) is contrapuntal, unaccompanied (the piano's bare octaves function as another voice in the polyphony), and filled with plaintive dissonances.

In the closing portion of the piece, a long process of decreasing activity accompanies the repeated last two lines of text, symbolizing the approach of slumber. Beginning in m. 42 the piano's afterbeats are sustained and the bass pattern is reduced to its second measure only, always with a falling octave F. Rests invade both the afterbeats and the vocal parts in mm. 45–46, and the piano leaves "Schlummerlied" to the voices alone. When it resumes, *pianissimo,* the afterbeats have been replaced by chords of two beats' duration, beginning on the weak beat and with the falling octave F as an ostinato pedal point. As before, rests appear in both the accompaniment and the vocal lines (their melody now a third lower), and once more "Schlummerlied" is unaccompanied. The postlude recalls the earlier ostinato-like bass figure in augmentation to provide a tranquil conclusion. Its first half combines right-hand afterbeats (now quarter notes) with a reminiscence of the voices' sighing figure; of the second half, only the falling octave remains, the afterbeats enlarged to half measures and leading to a final sonorous arpeggio in the low register.

Theodor Billroth, in the letter cited above, remarked of "Abendlied" and the preceding "Spätherbst" that "one should hear things of that sort with a choir hidden in a garden at dusk."

Warum? Op. 92/4 (Why?)

Text by Johann Wolfgang von Goethe (1749–1832)

Warum doch erschallen	Why then do songs
Himmelwärts die Lieder?—	sound forth toward heaven?—
Zögen gerne nieder	They would like to pull down
Sterne, die droben	the stars that twinkle
Blinken und wallen,	and float up there,
Zögen sich Luna's	attract to themselves Luna's
Lieblich Umarmen,	loving embrace,
Zögen die warmen,	entice down to us
Wonnigen Tage	the warm, rapturous
Seliger Götter	days of the
Gern uns herab!	blessed gods!

B♭ major; common time, *Lebhaft* (lively)/⁶⁄₈, *Anmutig bewegt* (gracefully animated); SATB.

Approximate duration: 2′05.

Two contrasting sections with some shared material.

Probably composed during summer 1884, although the details are unclear. A letter dated 6 August 1884 from Billroth to Brahms acknowledges receipt of several manuscripts, among them "quartets with piano accompaniment," of which "you seem to have given the palm to the verse of Goethe. . . . The melodic answer to the somewhat rhythmically and harmonically restless question satisfies one."

The first performances of "Warum?" and "Spätherbst" (Op. 92/2) were sung (together with "O schöne Nacht" [Op. 92/1]) on 4 February 1889 in Frankfurt am Main.

The text is from a curtain-raiser ("Was wir bringen") for the 1802 opening of a new theater in Lauchstädt.

Like the "songs" of the text, dominant harmonies in a vigorous dotted rhythm "sound forth toward heaven" in the introduction, only to sidestep at the last instant to the key of the lowered submediant—often Brahms's key for the realm of imagination—for the entrance of the voices. The soprano has the first in a series of fugal entrances of a subject marked by an initial descending arpeggio followed by a seventh leap upward. Each statement is accompanied by another dotted-rhythm rise in the piano that leads to the next entrance. The soprano moves from G♭ major to B major;

the alto (m. 5), from B major to C major; the bass (m. 8), from C major to F major; and the tenor (m. 10), from F major to the tonic B♭ major. Small wonder that Billroth found the section "harmonically restless"! But the music becomes quieter after the tenor's entrance, and his statement is accompanied only by a throbbing dominant pedal. A new accompaniment in flowing eighth notes leads through an augmented-sixth harmony to D major and on to an expectant unharmonized D just before the double bar— the musical equivalent of the two repetitions of "die Lieder" with their question marks.

The tenor in m. 13 has sung the word "himmelwärts" to an almost unnoticed motive comprising a broken tonic triad and a turn to E♭ plus a skip downward; the same motive is immediately sung twice more by the soprano in mm. 14–16. At the change to $\frac{6}{8}$, a variant of this motive becomes the basis of "the melodic answer" to which Billroth referred.

The new section is gracefully lyric and mostly homophonic with an accompaniment in wide-ranging sixteenth-note arpeggios, the piano sometimes contributing melodically as well. "Luna's lieblich Umarmen" and "seliger Götter" elicit turns to G♭ major and D major respectively, both keys having been prominently predicted in the first section. Occasional separate pairing of the female and male voices leads to full-fledged canonic writing in pairs for the closing repetitions of "gern uns herab!"

The piano's frequent isolated rising arpeggios in the $\frac{6}{8}$ section are an almost constant metaphoric reminder of the rising songs that are the subject of the entire work.

Zigeunerlieder

OPUS 103 (GYPSY SONGS)

TRANSLATED FROM THE HUNGARIAN BY HUGO CONRAT (DATES UNKNOWN)

Zigeunerlieder für vier Singstimmen (Sopran, Alt, Tenor und Bass) mit Begleitung des Pianoforte von Johannes Brahms (Gypsy songs for four solo voices [soprano, alto, tenor, and bass] with piano accompaniment by Johannes Brahms), Op. 103. Score and parts published in October 1888 by N. Simrock in Berlin; publication numbers 9026 (score) and 8979 (parts); score with German text, parts with text in both German and English.

The immediate popularity of the eleven quartets led to Simrock's publication of nos. 1–7 and 11 for solo voice and piano in April/May 1889. The keys for high voice (publication number 9046) are those of the quartet version except that no. 7 is a semitone higher, in E major; the low-key transpositions (publication number 9047) are inconsistent, major or minor thirds lower.

Approximate duration of the entire set: 16′10.

Composed during winter 1887/88 in Vienna.

The texts are translations of Hungarian folk songs attributed to the Viennese businessman Hugo Conrat. Actually, according to Kalbeck, Fräulein Witzl, a Hungarian-born nanny employed in Conrat's house, made the German translations and Conrat worked them into rhymed verse (*Johannes Brahms,* IV$_1$, 95). The German versions were published in *Ungarische Liebeslieder. 25 ungarische Volkslieder für mittlere Stimme. Die Klavierbegleitung von Zoltán Nagy* (Hungarian love songs. Twenty-five Hungarian folk songs for medium voice. The piano accompaniments by Zoltán Nagy) (Budapest and Leipzig, no date).

Conrat brought the poems to the attention of Brahms, the composer of the widely popular Hungarian Dances, and after a brief winter holiday in Budapest, Brahms set eagerly to work. In a short time the eleven *Zigeuner-lieder* were ready for a reading by the circle of Brahms's friends for whom they were intended. This first informal performance took place at the home of Ignaz Brüll, where Fräulein Witzl was then employed; characteristically, Brahms insisted that she, as the "originator" (*Urheber*) of the Gypsy Songs, be brought down from the nursery to the music room for the occasion. The singers were Minna Walter (daughter of Gustav), Hermine Schwarz (Ignaz Brüll's sister), Gustav Walter (a famed tenor of the Viennese court opera, who sang first performances of many of Brahms's Lieder), and Max Kalbeck, with Brahms and Brüll alternating at the piano (Kalbeck, *Johannes Brahms*, IV_1, 94ff.)

The first public performance was sung by Frau Schmidt-Köhne, Amalie Joachim, Raimund von Zur Mühlen, and Felix Schmidt on 31 October 1888 at the Singakademiesaal in Berlin. There were earlier private performances in March or April 1888 at Billroth's house in Vienna and on 15 October at Julius Stockhausen's in Frankfurt am Main—a performance at which Clara Schumann was present (see below).

Just as the *Liebeslieder* find inexhaustible inspiration in the $\frac{3}{4}$ lilt of the *Ländler* and waltz, so do the *Zigeunerlieder* exalt the $\frac{2}{4}$ csárdás; though the tempo changes, the meter does not. Only rarely is there a hint of the original Hungarian folk melodies, and even these instances are perceptible more as influence than as quotation. Yet there is an undeniable aura of authentic ethnicity, the result of frequent phrase lengths of other than four measures, the balancing of unlike phrases, a wide range of tempos, great rhythmic vitality and freshness, the alternation of major and minor mode within a single number, and an occasional suggestion of folk instruments. In the original quartet version, there is an extraordinary exploitation of color in the scoring for voices.

The originality of the Gypsy Songs and Brahms's fondness for them gave rise to an unusual amount of correspondence with those who customarily had an early look at new works. In April 1888, Brahms wrote to Clara Schumann from Vienna:

> At Billroth's we had a very pleasant evening with the *Zigeunerlieder* for quartet with piano. . . . They are a sort of Hungarian *Liebeslieder*, and beautifully sung as they were and in such jolly company, you would have found listening to them a delight. Otherwise they might seem to you a little too rollicking. . . . If only Stockhausen had a fine quartet I would come and have them sung to you.

On 5 May he referred to them again:

> As to the *Zigeunerlieder*, for the moment the matter is off. Simrock is here and I have allowed him to get them out of me. I should have liked you to see them beforehand, as usual, but it is perhaps better so. In any case playing them through is not enough for you, and an experiment with

Stockhausen and the quartet would in all probability have failed. . . . I do not think that these rollicking and unpretentious pieces would altogether please you, but you would have really enjoyed hearing them sung, as they were the other day, at the Tonkünstler-Verein by a really excellent quartet.

On 16 October Clara sent word to Brahms from Frankfurt:

I must send you a short but hearty letter of thanks today for your *Zigeunerlieder*, which I at last heard yesterday most perfectly performed at Stockhausen's. Everyone sang with genuine enthusiasm . . . and I enjoyed them immensely. If only I could have heard them again today so as to get to know one or two of them more thoroughly and pick out my favorite. Thus the parcel from Simrock has been a double pleasure to me—I have just received everything, even the precious portfolios of songs. [Simrock had also published the Lieder Opp. 105–107 in October 1888.] Unfortunately, however, the singing parts to the *Zigeunerlieder* are missing. Could you have them sent to me?

Brahms to Clara, 19 October:

I wrote to Simrock at once to send you the parts. . . . They must have been very beautifully sung to have won your favor!

Clara to Brahms, 4 November:

Today we are again going to hear the *Zigeunerlieder* at Stockhausen's (he is giving a song recital) which I am much looking forward to.

And again the next day, 5 November, Clara to Brahms:

I feel I must follow up my letter of yesterday with another, as I must unburden my heart of the joy your *Zigeunerlieder* have given me. I am quite delighted with them. How original they are and how full of freshness, charm and passion! How wonderful the voice progression is, so graceful and full of interest! Their feeling is so varied that in spite of the incessant $\frac{2}{4}$ time one is not conscious of any monotony. . . . The enthusiasm was great and many of the songs had to be repeated. . . . Let me press your hand, dear giver of joys.

Brahms responded on 6 November:

I was charmed to hear that the *Zigeuner* had afforded you so much pleasure.

Having hinted earlier at "some excessively gay stuff of mine, which a few people here are very fond of singing and hearing," Brahms sent the *Zigeunerlieder* in manuscript to Elisabeth von Herzogenberg on 11 March 1888 with a note:

I should be glad to think the enclosed has provided you with an hour's amusement, but I fear the humor will prove too violent in the quiet, subdued atmosphere of your room. [Elisabeth's husband, Heinrich, was confined to his bed by a crippling ailment of his right leg that eluded diagnosis and finally required surgery.] But apart from that, I wonder whether you will dislike the things? In any case, please keep them quite to yourselves. When you return them, I shall certainly be able to respond with some small things that are less crude.

Elisabeth responded two weeks later, on 25 March:

Your songs were a great pleasure. . . . Send something else soon. Please tell me where you found the words. The line of the melodies often strikes me as being more Bohemian-Dvořákesque than Hungarian.

The Herzogenbergs received copies of the newly published *Zigeunerlieder,* the Op. 104 part-songs, and the Lieder Opp. 105–107 in Nice, where Heinrich was convalescing. Elisabeth wrote to Brahms on 13 October 1888:

Your delightful big parcel of music came today, and will soon produce a letter in which I shall say anything that comes first, just as I feel it. How splendid to have all this pile to look through and appropriate to oneself! I value the *Zigeunerlieder* twice as much for having seen them in undress first. If you would but give me that pleasure oftener!

The promised letter of spontaneous reactions followed two weeks later on 28 October, and it included the following remarks about the Gypsy Songs:

The more I play the *Zigeunerlieder,* the more I love them. . . . They are so gloriously alive—rushing throbbing stamping along, then settling down to a smooth, gentle flow. We cannot try them properly in this beautiful uncivilized spot [Nice], and it is a sore deprivation. Yet I have a vivid idea of how they all sound. . . . How delightful it would be to arrange a really good performance of this fine work by a few music-lovers! I look forward to next winter for this sort of enjoyment.

Brahms replied on 3 November 1888 in the self-deprecating tone with which he customarily acknowledged compliments:

[I did] not expect to hear you say such nice things about the *Zigeunerlieder.* I prefer to consider it an error of judgment rather than a case of hypocrisy, however, so for the present accept my sincere though hasty thanks.

Theodor Billroth, who had become intimately acquainted with the quartets in manuscript, wrote upon receipt of his prepublication copy (22 August 1888):

I am delighted with this opus of yours and enjoy myself often with the freshness and the warmth of these glorious songs.

1.

He, Zigeuner, greife in die Saiten ein,	Hey, Gypsy, set bow to strings!
Spiel' das Lied vom ungetreuen Mägdelein!	Play the song of the unfaithful lass!
Laß die Saiten weinen, klagen traurig bange,	Let the strings, sadly anxious, weep and lament
Bis die heiße Träne netzet diese Wange!	until hot tears moisten these cheeks!

A minor; *Allegro agitato–Più Presto;* SATB.

Approximate duration: 1′30.

Rounded binary, with a coda *(Più Presto)* that restates all of the preceding material; A A′ B B′ A″ B″.

Like drumbeats introducing the dance, the piano begins with a re-bounding figure in sixteenth notes that will underlie the entire body of the piece, conflicting with the right hand's oscillating triplets. The tenor alone has a soaring, wide-ranging melody comprising two six-measure phrases and moving from tonic to dominant. The four voices repeat in homophonic style, the melody in the soprano.

A similar section ensues, the tenor solo now having phrases of eight measures (tonic major to dominant) and seven measures, the piano adding a balancing eighth measure (tonic major to tonic major). Noteworthy are the sobbing appoggiaturas at "weinen, klagen, traurig" in mm. 29–31 and the brief return of the opening melody, reharmonized, at m. 35. Again the four voices repeat in homophonic style.

A tiny piano interlude abandons the sixteenth-note drumbeat figure, restores the tonic minor, and leads to the coda with an abrupt full cadence in *forte.* Over a chordal triplet figure in the accompaniment, tossed agitatedly from hand to hand, the four voices recapitulate the melodies of both of the preceding sections. The harmonies are essentially unchanged, though the voicing is somewhat varied.

The postlude fades away as major yields to minor, only to end with the same abrupt cadence in *forte* that introduced the coda. (The solo song version lacks the entire coda and ends softly.)

2.

Hochgetürmte Rimaflut, wie bist du so trüb',	High-towered Rima river, how forlorn you are;
An dem Ufer klag' ich laut nach dir, mein Lieb!	on the bank I grieve aloud for you, my love!
Wellen fliehen, Wellen strömen,	Waves recede, waves stream by,
Rauschen an den Strand heran zu mir;	rush up to me at the river's edge;
An dem Rimaufer laßt mich ewig weinen nach ihr!	on the banks of the Rima let me weep for her forever!

D minor; *Allegro molto;* SATB.

Approximate duration: 1′15.
Rounded binary.
In line 3, Ophüls gives "fließen" (flow) instead of "fliehen" (recede).

The opening section comprises two seven-measure homophonic phrases, each extended to eight measures by the piano; the second section, also homophonic, has a ten-measure phrase and an eight-measure phrase extended to nine. A two-measure tonic-major harmony in the piano's low register serves as a postlude.

Both phrases in the first section begin in unison before blossoming into four-part harmony; when the same melody is recalled in m. 27, the bass and soprano sing in unison while the inner voices provide harmonic support. The opening motive reappears in the chromatic bass line at the beginning of the second section to support the succession of dominant and diminished sevenths that suggests the movement of waves. The grace note that appears in the soprano in mm. 6, 14, and 33 (imitated by the piano in mm. 8, 16, and 35) sounds "authentic" while evoking the forlornness, grieving, and weeping of the text.

3.

Wißt ihr, wann mein Kindchen	Do you know when my little darling
Am allerschönsten ist?	is at her most beautiful?
Wenn ihr süßes Mündchen	When her dear little mouth
Scherzt und lacht und küßt.	jokes and laughs and kisses.
Mägdelein,	Sweet lass,
Du bist mein,	you are mine,

Inniglich	I kiss you
Küß' ich dich,	tenderly,
Dich erschuf der Himmel	heaven created you
Einzig nur für mich.	just for me alone!
Wißt ihr, wann mein Liebster	Do you know when my lover
Am besten mir gefällt?	pleases me most?
Wenn in seinen Armen	When he holds me
Er mich umschlungen hält.	clasped tightly in his arms.
Schätzelein,	My precious,
Du bist mein,	you are mine,
Inniglich	I kiss you
Küß' ich dich,	tenderly,
Dich erschuf der Himmel	heaven created you
Einzig nur für mich!	just for me alone!

D major; *Allegretto-Allegro;* SATB.

Approximate duration: 1′15.

Strophic.

Each strophe comprises an *Allegretto* solo section in *piano* and an *Allegro* section for the four voices that begins and ends in *forte*. The solo segment consists of two four-measure phrases, the second extended to five by the piano, and is sung by the tenor in strophe 1 but by the soprano in strophe 2. The repeated *Allegro* has a homophonic four-measure phrase and a five-measure phrase for paired voices (SA + TB), which is extended to six measures by the piano.

The piano is given a four-measure interlude between strophes and a two-measure punctuation that serves as postlude. Noteworthy are the wrong-octave imitations of the solo voice's dotted-rhythm motive, the bubbling sixteenth notes in the *Allegro,* and the decrease of rhythmic activity to silence in the interlude.

4.

Lieber Gott, du weißt, wie oft bereut	Dear God, you know how often I
ich hab',	have regretted
Daß ich meinem Liebsten einst ein	that I once gave my sweetheart a
Küßchen gab.	little kiss.
Herz gebot, daß ich ihn küssen muß,	My heart commanded me to kiss him;
Denk', so lang' ich leb', an diesen	I will remember that first kiss as long as
ersten Kuß.	I live.

Lieber Gott, du weißt, wie oft in
    stiller Nacht
Ich in Lust und Leid an meinen Schatz
    gedacht.
Lieb' ist süß, wenn bitter auch
    die Reu',
Armes Herze bleibt mir ewig,
    ewig treu.

Dear God, you know how often in
    the quiet night
I, in joy and pain, have thought of my
    sweetheart.
Love is sweet, though remorse is
    bitter;
my poor heart will remain forever,
    forever true.

F major; *Vivace grazioso;* SATB.

Approximate duration: 1′00.
Strophic.

Each strophe comprises two four-measure phrases for soprano solo, each leading from tonic to dominant, and a repeated pair of four-measure phrases for all four voices, the first leading to a cadence on the dominant, the second wending its way back to the tonic. The solo is entirely in *piano;* each of the four-voice phrases begins homophonically and *forte* but proceeds in *piano* with the men's and women's voices treated as separate pairs.

The overall tone is animated and playful; the only touch of darkness is provided by the minor harmonies in mm. 13–14 for "denk', so lang' ich leb' " in verse 1, "armes Herze bleibt" in verse 2. Both the bar of silence in the piano interlude and the sudden *forte* of the final chord add an element of surprise.

5.

Brauner Bursche führt zum Tanze
Sein blauäugig schönes Kind,
Schlägt die Sporen keck zusammen,
Czardas-Melodie beginnt;
Küßt und herzt sein süßes Täubchen,
Dreht sie, führt sie, jauchzt und
    springt!
Wirft drei blanke Silbergulden
Auf das Cimbal, daß es klingt.

    A tanned youth leads his beautiful
blue-eyed girl to the dance,
strikes his spurs together boldly,
a csárdás melody begins;
he kisses and embraces his sweet dove,
twirls her, leads her, cheers and
    leaps!
He throws three shiny silver coins
onto the cymbal to make it clang.

D major; *Allegro giocoso;* SATB.

Approximate duration: 1′15.
Strophic; the entire song is sung twice.

The eloquent two-measure introduction bespeaks the piano's importance in the progress of this lovely piece. There are four six-measure
phrases, the first, second, and fourth of which share the same rhythm and
cede their final two measures to the piano alone. The third phrase suddenly begins *piano* despite the prevailing *forte;* to a new rhythm, the voices
sing all six measures, gradually regaining the *forte* and ending with a *fermata*
on a dominant-seventh chord.

The voices are treated homophonically throughout. In the postlude,
the suspenseful *fermata* of the introduction (and the interlude) is at last
replaced by a welcome tonic chord.

6.

Röslein dreie in der Reihe blüh'n so rot, Daß der Bursch' zum Mädel geht, ist kein Verbot! Lieber Gott, wenn das verboten wär', Ständ' die schöne weite Welt schon längst nicht mehr, Ledig bleiben Sünde wär'!	Three little roses in a row bloom so red; there is no law against a youth's visiting a girl! Dear God, if that were prohibited, the beautiful, wide world would long ago have ceased to exist; to remain single would be a sin!
Schönstes Städtchen in Alföld ist Ketschkemet, Dort gibt es gar viele Mädchen schmuck und nett! Freunde, sucht euch dort ein Bräutchen aus, Freit um ihre Hand und gründet euer Haus, Freudenbecher leeret aus!	The nicest little town in Alföld is Kecskemét; there are truly a lot of trim and nice girls there! Friends, find yourselves a little bride there, ask for her hand and establish your line, drain the cup of joy!

G major; *Vivace grazioso;* SATB.

Approximate duration: 1′20.
Strophic, the strophe binary.

After a tiny introduction, the solo tenor begins with two cheery four-measure phrases; in their immediate repetition by the upper three voices, the last two bars are slightly altered in order to end on the dominant instead of the tonic, and the piano adds downward-rippling sixteenth notes at the cadence bars.

The sixteenths turn upward to accompany the first and third of the three four-measure phrases in the repeated B section, all scored for four voices. The middle phrase reverts to the earlier rhythm and accompaniment style. Some secondary dominants and a nod at the minor subdominant provide contrast to the prevailing diatonic harmony. The short last line of the poetic verse contributes to the effect of Brahms's characteristic broadening of the last phrase.

The piano echoes the final vocal phrase to serve either (with last measure silent) as interlude between the strophes or (proceeding to tonic harmony) as postlude.

Elisabeth von Herzogenberg remarked on the "charming humor" of no. 6, the critic Eduard Hanslick on its "playful mockery" and "delicacy."

7.

Kommt dir manchmal in den Sinn,	Do you sometimes remember,
Mein süßes Lieb,	my sweet love,
Was du einst mit heil'gem Eide	what you once promised me
Mir gelobt?	with a solemn oath?
Täusch' mich nicht, verlaß' mich nicht,	Don't deceive me, don't desert me,
Du weißt nicht, wie lieb ich dich hab',	you don't know how fond of you I am;
Lieb' du mich, wie ich dich,	love me as I love you,
Dann strömt Gottes Huld auf dich	then God's grace will stream down
herab.	on you.

E♭ major; *Andantino grazioso;* SATB.

Approximate duration: 1'30.
Binary.
Each of the tenor's opening three-measure phrases is extended to four by the piano. For the slightly elaborated repetition by all four voices, the piano adds right-hand afterbeats and more active counterpoint in its solo measures.

The second part has two five-measure phrases for the tenor, repeated with some contrapuntal independence by the four voices. The piano's sixteenth notes often seem to echo the melody in diminution—in the second phrase there is additional imitation between right and left hands.

In contrast to the spirit, vigor, and humor of the preceding numbers, no. 7 has the intimate air of a heartfelt love song, aided by its tender appoggiaturas and its occasionally lowered sixth scale degree. In her letter to Brahms of 28 October 1888, Elisabeth von Herzogenberg spoke of its "adorable melancholy fervor" and added, "I am always moved to tears in the second part."

8.

Horch, der Wind klagt in den Zweigen traurig sacht.	Hark, the wind laments softly and sadly in the branches;
Süßes Lieb, wir müssen scheiden: gute Nacht.	sweet love, we must part: good night.
Ach, wie gern in deinen Armen ruhte ich,	Oh, how gladly I rested in your arms,
Doch die Trennungsstunde naht, Gott schütze dich.	But the hour of parting nears; may God protect you.
Dunkel ist die Nacht, kein Sternlein spendet Licht;	The night is dark, no little star gives light;
Süßes Lieb, vertrau' auf Gott und weine nicht.	sweet love, trust in God and don't cry.
Führt der liebe Gott mich einst zu dir zurück,	Once the dear Lord leads me back to you,
Bleiben ewig wir vereint in Liebesglück.	we will remain united forever in lovers' bliss.

G minor/major; *Andante semplice;* SATB.

Approximate duration: 1′45.
Strophic.

The first two lines of each stanza are set to music in the minor; the second two, more reassuring, are in the major. Tenor, alto, and soprano in turn have fugal entrances of a three-measure subject whose sinuous shape and chromaticism create what Elisabeth von Herzogenberg termed the section's "strange coloring." But the piano is given the fourth statement as the bass enters in homophony with the other voices.

The major section, by contrast, is more transparent in texture and diatonic in harmony. The third line of text is set to a three-measure phrase in eighth notes for solo tenor; the fourth line has an answering eighth-note melody for the soprano (supported by the other voices, mostly in quarters) that spans four measures and is extended to six by text repetition.

Closing music for the piano twice echoes the end of the vocal melody, in the treble and in the alto range. It returns to the minor as interlude before the second strophe, but it remains major as quiet postlude.

9.

Weit und breit schaut Niemand mich an,	Far and wide no one looks at me,
Und wenn sie mich hassen, was liegt mir d'ran?	and if they hate me, what does it matter to me?
Nur mein Schatz, der soll mich lieben allezeit,	If only my darling will love me forever,
Soll mich küssen, umarmen und herzen in Ewigkeit.	will kiss me, hug and embrace me through eternity.
Kein Stern blickt in finsterer Nacht;	No star appears in the gloomy night;
Keine Blum' mir strahlt in duftiger Pracht.	no flower envelops me in fragrant glory.
Deine Augen sind mir Blumen, Sternenschein,	Your eyes are flowers to me, and starlight,
Die mir leuchten so freundlich, die blühen nur mir allein.	that shine on me so amiably, that blossom for me alone.

G minor/major; *Allegro/Più Presto;* SATB.

Approximate duration: 1'40.

Strophic; the strophe, modified binary.

The voices and piano treble in unison begin each phrase of the opening repeated eight-measure period, trailed by the piano bass a half beat later. The chaotic rhythms of the section effectively portray the unease reflected in the first half of each stanza of text. Since the period modulates to the dominant of the relative major, a four-measure transition phrase ("Nur mein Schatz") is inserted to effect the further modulation to the tonic major as well as to moderate the rhythmic activity.

The *Più Presto* also comprises a repeated period, this time balancing a four-measure phrase with one of six measures. Although no modulation is necessary, a reharmonization of the transitional "Nur mein Schatz" melody is inserted before the repetition, perhaps to provide harmonic variety. Taking a cue from its longer note values, the tenor begins the recurrence of the period with a quarter-note skeletal version of his earlier line.

The G-major section seems to have been suggested by the first stanza of the text. The steady eighths of the four-measure phrase constitute a metaphor for "lieben allezeit"; after the rest-separated list of activities associated with that love in the six-measure phrase, the slowed pace of the cadence illustrates "in Ewigkeit."

The piano's first ending prepares for the minor-mode beginning of the second strophe; the second presses on to a joyous conclusion.

In line 5, Ophüls gives "blinkt" (twinkles) instead of "blickt."

10.

Mond verhüllt sein Angesicht,	The moon covers its face;
Süßes Lieb, ich zürne dir nicht.	sweet love, I am not angry with you.
Wollt' ich zürnend dich betrüben,	Were I in anger to cause you distress,
Sprich, wie könnt' ich dich dann	tell me, how then could I also love you?
lieben?	
Heiß für dich mein Herz entbrennt,	My heart burns hotly for you,
Keine Zunge dir's bekennt.	[though] no tongue admits it to you.
Bald in Liebesrausch unsinnig,	Sometimes I am in an insane transport
	of love,
Bald wie Täubchen sanft und innig.	sometimes as gentle and tender as a
	little dove.

B♭ major; *Andantino;* SATB.

Approximate duration: 2′20.

Strophic, the strophe A A B.

The setting is marked by its fervor, its use nearly throughout of the female and male voices as separate pairs, and its imitations in the piano of the alternating-tone hammering of cimbalom mallets.

A quality of impassioned improvisation results from the extraordinary absence of predictability of both phrase structure and harmonic movement. Three-measure phrases predominate but are obscured by overlapping phrases in the other voice pair and by two-measure insertions in the piano; an effect of increasing phrase length accompanies the gradual dynamic decrease toward the end of the strophe. The initial tonic harmony is already made a dominant in the second measure, and the voices enter in what sounds like G minor, despite the B♮; the second phrase moves importantly toward D minor, and the final cadence borrows a G♭ from the tonic minor.

The stormy opening and quiet ending of the strophe reflect the emotional progression in each stanza of the text.

11.

Rote Abendwolken zieh'n
Am Firmament,
Sehnsuchtsvoll nach dir, mein Lieb,
Das Herze brennt;
Himmel strahlt in glüh'nder Pracht
Und ich träum' bei Tag und Nacht
Nur allein vom süßen Liebchen mein.

Red evening clouds drift by
in the firmament,
my heart smolders longingly
for you, my love;
the heavens shine in glowing splendor,
and I dream by day and night
only of my sweet darling.

D♭ major; *Allegro passionato;* SATB.

Approximate duration: 1′15.

Binary.

Each large section comprises two phrases for the tenor that are repeated in a homophonic harmonization for all four voices. In the initial segment, the vocal phrases occupy six measures each but are extended to eight by the piano's introductory chords and prolongation of the cadence—the harmonized version sustains the voices too into the eighth bar. The third phrase repeats four measures sequentially and adds one measure of piano introduction and a three-measure extension (which the quartet sings), a total of twelve measures. The final phrase spans ten measures, of which the last three extend the cadence; the vocal melody now includes the introductory bar, which has heretofore been the sole property of the piano. The tenor phrase stretches into the second bar of the cadence extension; the four voices sing all three. (The version for vocal solo adds two measures of tonic harmony for the piano at the end, thus increasing the closing phrase to twelve measures to balance phrase 3.)

A high level of emotional intensity and the pulsating accompaniment evoke the "longing smoldering" and "glowing splendor" of the text. Even after repeated hearings, the interplay between the tonic D♭ major and the enharmonically related E major continues to delight the ear. The setting recalls no. 1 of the cycle in its alternation of tenor solo with quartet and in the dotted rhythm, stepwise motion, and falling cadence of its opening melody.

Six Quartets

OPUS 112

Sechs Quartette für Sopran, Alt, Tenor, Bass mit Pianoforte von Johannes Brahms (Six quartets for soprano, alto, tenor, and bass with piano by Johannes Brahms), Op. 112. Score and parts published in November 1891 by C. F. Peters in Leipzig; publication numbers 7639 (score) and 7640 (parts); German text only.

The two Kugler settings and the four new *Zigeunerlieder* seem an odd collection, with reason. Though the quartets were prepared for publication during spring 1891 at Ischl, all six were probably composed earlier. For several years, Brahms had talked from time to time of giving up composition, and when he completed the G-major string quintet, Op. 111, in 1890, he declared it his last work. In 1891 he made a will (in a letter to Simrock) and began sorting through his unpublished manuscripts, salvaging those things he considered worthy of publication and destroying the rest. As a consequence, some of his publications during this compositional hiatus seem to be anthologies rather than organic works, this opus among them.

In June 1891, Brahms wrote to Clara Schumann from Ischl:

> It is wonderfully beautiful and pleasant here, and, as I have often said before, I am made most happy by the charming people about me. Of the many and sundry musical fancies that flit through my brain not much will survive, though a little may. And if, for example, in a week or so six solo quartets, including one piano part, should lie in fair copy before me I shall be tempted to send them to you, as I believe they might give you pleasure.

After her receipt of the six quartets in manuscript, Clara responded from Berchtesgaden, 15 August 1891:

> At last I have succeeded in snatching a quiet hour at the piano (only a very mediocre upright piano, it is true) and have revelled, albeit imperfectly, in the beauty of your songs. Once again they are the embodiment of all one could wish, and full of interest. Any singer might be proud of his voice in singing them, for he is everywhere so skillfully considered and, in spite of all their thoughtfulness, they are full of charm. I am particularly fond of the two first, the second notwithstanding its $\frac{5}{4}$ time which lends such mystic feeling to the whole. Of the *Zigeunerlieder,* the first is the one I like least. In the second I had to accustom myself to the ninth bar, but I like it, nevertheless, as well as the two others. If only we could hear them soon! Directly they are published I will get hold of [Julius] Stockhausen and see that he practices them at once. But that he will do without my having to tell him.

Sehnsucht, Op. 112/1 (Longing)

Text by Franz Theodor Kugler (1808–1858)

Es rinnen die Wasser Tag und Nacht,
    Deine Sehnsucht wacht.
	The waters run day and night,
	    your longing keeps watch.

Du gedenkest der vergangenen Zeit,
    Die liegt so weit.
	You remember a bygone time
	    that is so remote.

Du siehst hinaus in den Morgenschein
    Und bist allein.
	You look out into the morning light
	    and are alone.

Es rinnen die Wasser Tag und Nacht,
    Deine Sehnsucht wacht.
	The waters run day and night,
	    your longing keeps watch.

F minor; $\frac{2}{4}$; *Andante;* SATB.

Approximate duration: 3′00.
A B B′ A′.

Prepared for publication during spring 1891 but probably composed earlier. Kalbeck claims that all three of Brahms's settings of Kugler texts ("Serenade," Op. 106/1; "Sehnsucht"; and "Nächtens," Op. 112/2) date from the summer of 1888, when Brahms received from Kugler's daughter-in-law a copy of his 1830 *Skizzenbuch,* which included musical compositions and drawings in addition to poetry (*Johannes Brahms,* IV₁, 105–106).

The first performance is not documented.

The text appears in Kugler's *Gedichte* (Stuttgart and Tübingen, 1840).

The music is suffused with yearning, its chromatic language filled with aching dissonances, sustained diminished-seventh chords that often move on to other sevenths, and harmonies that circle rather than progressing. The piano introduction is an illustration in miniature: each painful attempt of the two voices to draw closer is followed by movement apart; the change to triplets in m. 3 increases the dissonance and agitation, but the same harmonic and melodic ground is traversed.

The frequent pairing of voices is a noteworthy feature here, as in "Nächtens," which follows.

The key scheme resembles that of a small sonata-allegro form. The introduction and first phrase are squarely in the tonic key; the men enter in m. 9 as though to echo the women, but their phrase instead forms a transition to the dominant. The first setting of "deine Sehnsucht wacht" is in the key of the dominant; the second is more ambiguous but arrives at G major, whose function as dominant of the dominant is made clear by the addition of its seventh in m. 25 as new material begins.

The setting of stanza 2 begins over a long G pedal. Melodically it grows out of a rising four-note chromatic scale and its free inversion. Harmonically, it consists almost entirely of seventh chords but finally arrives at a pure C major.

The music for stanza 3 resembles that of stanza 2, but its rising melodic motive is no longer completely chromatic and the inclusion of an upper neighbor expands it to five notes. Harmonically, its succession of seventh chords continues the function of a development section by avoiding the tonic while leading inevitably to its return in m. 57.

The setting of stanza 4, which is the same as stanza 1, constitutes a recapitulation and coda. The music of the introduction is recalled, and the men this time join the women in the first phrase, though they remain a separate pair of voices. That phrase, extended to six measures, remains in the key of the tonic, as now does the first setting of "deine Sehnsucht wacht." In its second setting, mm. 72–76, the crossing of the soprano and alto voices produces a variant of the piano's melody in the introduction and interlude. The final setting, with its octave leaps up to *forte* and down to *piano* and, anchored by a pedal point, its harmonic movement from diminished through half-diminished seventh to tonic major, seems to encapsulate both the unfulfilled longing of the piece and the wide range of the emotions that result.

Nächtens, Op. 112/2 (During the night)

Text by Franz Theodor Kugler (1808–1858)

Nächtens wachen auf die irren,	During the night arise the insane,
Lügenmächt'gen Spukgestalten,	illusory apparitions
Welche deinen Sinn verwirren.	that bewilder your senses.
Nächtens ist im Blumengarten	During the night hoarfrost fell
Reif gefallen, daß vergebens	in the flower garden, so that
Du der Blumen würdest warten.	you would wait in vain for blossoms.
Nächtens haben Gram und Sorgen	During the night grief and anxiety
In dein Herz sich eingenistet,	established themselves in your heart,
Und auf Tränen blickt der Morgen.	and the morning looks upon tears.

D minor; $\frac{5}{4}$; *Unruhig bewegt* (restlessly agitated); SATB.

Approximate duration: 1′35.

Varied strophic, with the effect of A B A′.

The date of composition is uncertain; prepared for publication spring 1891, but possibly composed summer 1888. (See the comments on "Sehnsucht," Op. 112/1, preceding.)

The first performance took place on 28 September 1895 during a music festival in Meiningen.

The text is found in Kugler's *Gedichte* (Stuttgart and Tübingen, 1840).

The setting is a night piece, but not the usual serene nocturne. It portrays instead a malevolent night, a night of madness and destruction, unease and dread. The atmosphere of foreboding is set by its restless $\frac{5}{4}$ meter (unique among these duets and quartets) and its quaking accompaniment.

The introductory piano motive frames each strophe and is the basis for the principal vocal melody, to which the first two lines of each stanza are sung in unison by the alto and bass. (In strophe 1 a slower-moving melody for the soprano and tenor, mostly in ghostly *sotto voce* unison, introduces and accompanies the main melody.) The third line of text, its initial melody consisting almost entirely of eighth notes, is set in each strophe with increasing complexity and with more repetitions, so that strophe 1 (after its vocal introduction) spans five measures; strophe 2, six; and strophe 3, seven.

Strophe 2 modulates to B♭ major. Strophe 3 implies a turn toward G minor and works up to an affecting climax in m. 18 before decreasing activity leads to a quiet ending.

The piano postlude continues the effect of broadening by modifying the $\frac{5}{4}$ meter, which has always been divided $\frac{2}{4} + \frac{3}{4}$, into two measures of each. The low-register ending, with its mournful appoggiaturas and final turn to the major, suggests the cheerless morning at night's end.

Vier Zigeunerlieder, Op. 112/3–6 (Four gypsy songs)
Translated from the Hungarian by Hugo Conrat (dates unknown)

The date of composition is uncertain. The songs were prepared for publication during spring 1891 at Ischl, but Brahms had known the texts since winter 1887/88, when the Op. 103 *Zigeunerlieder* were composed; these may date from the same period.

The four *Zigeunerlieder* of Op. 112 were first performed in Hamburg on 21 November 1892 at a subscription concert by members of the Cäcilienverein, Julius Spengel, conductor.

The texts were published in *Ungarische Liebeslieder. 25 ungarische Volkslieder für mittlere Stimmen. Die Klavierbegleitung von Zoltán Nagy* (Hungarian love songs. Twenty-five Hungarian folk songs for medium voice. The piano accompaniments by Zoltán Nagy) (Budapest and Leipzig, no date).

As in the Op. 103 set, all four quartets are in $\frac{2}{4}$ meter, and the balancing of unequal phrase lengths and the occasional suggestion of ethnic instruments are characteristic.

1. [Op. 112/3]

Himmel strahlt so helle und klar,	The sky shines so bright and clear;
Heller strahlt mir dein Augenpaar.	your two eyes shine on me more brightly.
Du meine Rose, mir in's Auge blick',	You, my rose, look into my eyes,
Daß ich dich segne in meinem Glück.	that I may bless you in my happiness.
Vögeleins Lied so lieblich erklingt,	The birdling's song rings out so sweetly;
Süß'res Lied mir mein Liebchen singt.	my sweetheart sings a sweeter song to me.
Du meine Rose, mir in's Auge blick'.	You, my rose, look into my eyes,
Daß ich dich segne in meinem Glück.	that I may bless you in my happiness.
Sonne küßt das ganze Erdenrund,	The sun kisses the entire wide world;
Heißer küßt mich dein Rosenmund.	your rosy mouth kisses me more hotly.
Du meine Rose, mir in's Auge blick',	You, my rose, look into my eyes,
Daß ich dich segne in meinem Glück.	that I may bless you in my happiness.

D major; *Allegro non troppo;* SATB.

Approximate duration: 1'30.
Strophic, slightly varied.

Brahms translates poetic lines of four feet into musical phrases of alternately four and seven measures. The *forte* opening pair follows a one-measure piano introduction that has an obvious kinship to "Rote Abendwolken zieh'n," Op. 103/11. A new accompaniment figure in *piano*, evocative of a concertina plus drone, overlaps the cadence, provides a measure of interlude, and gives rise to the second pair of phrases, which begin and end *piano* but have an interior *forte* climax. The ensuing six-measure interlude elides the closing cadence and develops both of the piano's earlier solo materials.

The first half of strophe 2 omits the bass voice and is accompanied by an effective cimbalom-suggestive figure in the piano's upper register. The voices are given a new melody for the last four notes, the original having been partially usurped by the piano.

In strophe 3 the final phrase is extended from seven measures to twelve by means of augmentation and additional repetition of text. The quiet ending is contradicted by the piano's sonorous recalling of the initial character of the strophe.

2. [Op. 112/4]

Rote Rosenknospen	Red rosebuds
Künden schon des Lenzes Triebe.	already herald the burgeoning of spring.
Rosenrote Wangen	Rose-red cheeks
Deuten Mädchens erste Liebe.	indicate a maiden's first love.
Kleiner roter Vogel,	Little red bird,
Flieg' herab zur roten Rose!	fly down to the red rose!
Bursche geht zum ros'gen	The youth goes to caress
Mädchen kosen.	the blushing maiden.

F major; *Allegretto grazioso;* SATB.

Approximate duration: 1'00.

A A' B B' coda.

The poem comprises four sentences, each sentence cast in the form of a couplet. Each of the first three couplets has seven poetic feet, the fourth only five.

The first two couplets are set in two similar periods, each comprising a four-measure phrase and a five-measure phrase with cadences on the tonic and dominant, respectively. The vocal lines of the second five-measure phrase are somewhat varied, though the melodic rhythm is unchanged. The first period, which announces the coming of spring, has a lighthearted accompaniment of detached descending sixteenths and staccato afterbeat chords; the accompaniment of the second period looks similar, but its six-teenths are now sustained to join the left hand's second-beat quarter notes, and the five-bar phrase, which mentions "a maiden's first love," adds sigh-ing double appoggiaturas.

The settings of the third and fourth couplets are also akin, each having two measures of vigorous dotted rhythms moving from subdominant to dominant followed by four measures that begin and end with tonic har-mony. But awkwardnesses arise because of the shorter fourth couplet; the piano follows the two-plus-four-measure formula, but the voices have a four-measure phrase that bridges the piano's phrases and ends inconclusively on C octaves.

Characteristically, Brahms finds a solution for the resulting unsatisfying imbalance that is sheer perfection. In a coda of striking beauty, the short couplet is repeated to music for the voices alone, *piano* and *dolcissimo,* that takes up the C octaves left dangling earlier and proceeds to materials that meld the maiden's "rose-red cheeks" (mm. 10–13) with the youth's move-ment to caress her (mm. 25–28). The phrase is long enough to balance the periods that preceded it; its scoring for voices alone serves to complete the previous vocal phrase, seemingly interrupted by the piano, and bal-ances the sound of piano alone; its hushed dynamic and melodic reminis-cence form a connection with the beginning of the piece; and its effect of rhythmic augmentation gives it a touching quality of epilogue. The piano's final comment carries the melody satisfyingly to the upper tonic.

3. [Op. 112/5]

Brennessel steht am Weges Rand,	Nettles grow beside the path;
Neider und Feinde hab' ich in Stadt	I have enviers and enemies in town
und Land.	and countryside.
Neidet, haßt, verleumdet, doch das	Envy, hate, slander! that really causes
bringt mir keine Not!	me no distress,
Wenn mir nur mein süßes Liebchen	if only my sweet darling will remain
treu bleibt bis zum Tod.	true to me until death.

F minor/major; *Allegro;* SATB.

Approximate duration: 1'05.
Modified binary; A A transition B B'.

Brahms seems to find the metric irregularity of the poem more a source of inspiration than an obstacle.

Over a robust accompaniment of sixteenth-note triplets and staccato eighth-note chords, the initial phrases of four and five measures correspond to the four and five poetic feet of the poem's opening lines. The first phrase moves to Ab major, the second returns to the tonic.

But the seven feet of the long third line occupy eight measures of music, divided four plus four. "Neidet, haßt, verleumdet" elicits chromatic harmonies and a trenchant octave-doubled bass line with afterbeat chords. "Doch das bringt mir keine Not" reestablishes the earlier accompaniment figure and moves quickly from Ab major to C as dominant. Text repetitions accommodate yet another four-measure segment, which confirms the dominant; raises the third, sixth, and seventh scale steps; and allows the piano to recall the opening vocal motive while reducing its sixteenth-note groupings from six to truncated four.

The contrast between the harshness of the real world and the prospect of enduring love is marked by a change to the tonic major and the introduction of a caressing new accompaniment figure based on the incomplete groups of four sixteenths. The poem's unwieldy fourth line is set, first for tenor solo, then harmonized for all four voices, to an ingratiating melody in which no syllable until the last falls on a downbeat. The line seems to unroll seamlessly for thirteen measures, but the harmonic patterning in the accompaniment and the repetition of "treu bleibt bis zum Tod" reveal three groups of four, the last vocal phrase overlapping the beginning of the succeeding section.

In the postlude, the piano takes up the rhythm of the vocal melody, but it ends with punctuation that recalls the sixteenth-note triplet figure and vigorous style of the beginning.

4. [Op. 112/6]

Liebe Schwalbe, kleine Schwalbe,	Dear swallow, little swallow,
Trage fort mein kleines Briefchen!	carry forth my little letter!
Flieg' zur Höhe, fliege schnell aus,	Fly to the heights, fly away quickly,
Flieg' hinein in Liebchens Haus!	fly into my sweetheart's house!

Fragt man dich, woher du kommest,	If you're asked where you come from,
Wessen Bote du geworden,	whose messenger you have become,
Sag', du kommst vom treu'sten Herzen,	say you come from the most faithful heart,
Das vergeht in Trennungsschmerzen.	that is dying from the pain of separation.

D minor/major; *Presto;* SATB.

Approximate duration: 0′45.
Strophic.

The setting is introduced by the minor form of the supertonic-dominant progression that begins "Himmel strahlt so helle," Op. 112/3, and is so characteristic of "Rote Abendwolken zieh'n," Op. 103/11.

The entire first verse is set for alto solo, the second for alto and tenor duet, to music whose breathless pace and regular phrase structure give it the ring of authentic gypsy dance music; the incessant dotted quarter–eighth note rhythm without rests, however, is a potential source of breathing problems for the singers.

The last two lines of each verse are set a second time for the four voices in the major, to music which is pleasantly reminiscent of the second theme of no. 1 of these four *Zigeunerlieder,* Op. 112/3.

For the second strophe, the left hand of the accompaniment is considerably elaborated.

The postlude recalls the rhythm of the minor melody and concludes with *fermata* chords on supertonic and tonic that evoke, bookend style, the opening progression.

Little Wedding Cantata,

WoO POSTH. 16

TEXT BY GOTTFRIED KELLER (1819–1890)

Zwei Geliebte, treu verbunden,
Gehen durch die Welt spazoren,
Jedes hat sein Herz verloren,
Doch das andre hat's gefunden.

Jeder trägt die leichte Last
Wie die Uhr am Kettchen fast.
Also geht's auf Steg und Wegen
Ruhig fort mit gleichen Schlägen.

"Schau, die können's!" sagen ferne
An der Himmelshöh' die Sterne.
"Wer sind sie?" Gleich schrei'n
             wir da:
"Sigmund und Emilia!"

Two sweethearts, faithfully united,
stroll together through the world;
each has lost his heart,
but the other has found it.

Each one carries the light load
almost like a watch on its little chain.
So they calmly proceed on highway
and byway to the same beat.

"Look, they can do it!" say the
distant stars in the vault of heaven.
"Who are they?" Immediately we shout
             back,
"Sigmund and Emilia!"

F major; $\frac{3}{4}$; *Tempo di Menuetto;* SATB.

Approximate duration: 0'55.

Through-composed, though the opening melodic motive recurs at mm. 17–19 and 33–34. The overall form resembles rounded binary, without repetitions but with a coda.

Composed in July 1874 at Rüschlikon. Marie Exner had asked Keller for a wedding song for the marriage of her brother Sigmund to Emilie von Winiwarter. Brahms set the text to music at Keller's request, despite his lack of enthusiasm for the task. (His pocket calendar for 1874 shows the July entry "wedding joke.") In the letter accompanying the manuscript he begged Keller to "assume the responsibility for both words and music." Consequently Sigmund Exner was obliged to promise that no one would be allowed to copy the piece. It did not appear in print until 1927, when it was published in the Brahms *Sämtliche Werke*, ed. Eusebius Mandyczewski (Leipzig: Breitkopf & Härtel, no date), vol. 20, 226–28.

The work was first performed during the summer 1874 nuptial festivities of Sigmund and Emilie Exner.

The text is a humorous parody of the closing lines of Goethe's *Rinaldo;* it was printed in the Bächthold biography of Keller (Berlin, 1897).

With mock seriousness, the setting begins in the style of an eighteenth-century minuet. The accompaniment's bassoonlike staccato left hand suggests several of the text's images—the strolling couple, the lost-though-found hearts, the ticking watch, the shared beat to which the pair proceeds through life. The right hand's characteristic afterbeat chords yield to a *leggiero* dotted-rhythm figure in mm. 9–17, based on the initial vocal melody and evocative of the "light load" that each partner carries.

But the parodic element becomes amply apparent in the codalike setting of stanza 3. Stately trumpets accompany the pronouncement of the stars, whose distance elicits a turn to the foreign-sounding A♭ major. The stars themselves are portrayed in the piano's glistening high-register octaves in mm. 27–29, the accompaniment seemingly having detoured temporarily into awestruck duple meter. Quasi-orchestral interjections in the style of opera recitative punctuate "wer sind sie?" and "gleich schrei'n wir da" and lead the way back to the tonic key. There the response "Sigmund und Emilia!" (which twice spans four beats against the prevailing triple meter) is sung amid a clangor of bells, pealing in joyous celebration.

POETS AND TRANSLATORS

ALEXIS, WILLIBALD (pseudonym of Georg Wilhelm Häring; b. Breslau, 1798; d. Arnstadt [Thuringia], 1871). Writer and critic, best known for the historical novels in which he continually experimented with methods of presentation. He edited the *Berliner Konversationsblatt* from 1827 to 1835, contributed essays and reviews to literary journals, and wrote travel books. From 1842 until 1860 he was the principal editor of a thirty-volume collection of accounts of crimes, *Der neue Pitavel.*
Op. 75/4: "Walpurgisnacht"

ALLMERS, HERMANN (b. Rechenfleth bei Bremen, 1821; d. Rechenfleth, 1902). Essayist, dramatist, novelist, and poet primarily interested in legendary lore and nature. His best writing centers on description of the natural environment; his best-known works were *Marschenbuch* (1858) and *Römische Schlendertage* (1859). His collected works appeared in six volumes, 1891–1896.
Op. 92/2: "Spätherbst"

ARNIM, LUDWIG JOACHIM (ACHIM) VON (b. Berlin, 1781; d. Wiepersdorf, 1831). A leading Romantic poet who, with CLEMENS BRENTANO (b. Ehrenbreitstein, 1778; d. Aschaffenburg, 1842), also an important poet, published the influential early collection of folk poetry *Des Knaben Wunderhorn* (Heidelberg, 1806–1808). It in turn stimulated the publication of many additional collections of both folk poetry and folk melodies throughout the nineteenth century. From *Des Knaben Wunderhorn:*
Op. 66/5: "Hüt' du dich!"
Op. 75/2: "Guter Rat"

BRENTANO, CLEMENS. See ARNIM, LUDWIG JOACHIM (ACHIM) VON.

CANDIDUS, KARL (b. Bischweiler [Alsace], 1817; d. Feodosie [Crimea], 1872. Cleric, theologian, philosopher, and poet. He worked as a clergyman in Nancy and later in Odessa, but despite his travels he remained an ardent German patriot.
Op. 66/4: "Jägerlied"

CONRAT, HUGO (dates unknown). Cultured Viennese businessman and contributing correspondent for the *Neue Musikzeitung.* Charged with the translation of a group of Hungarian love songs into rhymed German for publication, he brought the resulting texts to Brahms's attention. Brahms subsequently became a frequent guest in his home. Conrat's daughter Ilse sculpted the marble monument for Brahms's Vienna grave site.

Op. 103: *Zigeunerlieder* (trans.)
1. He, Zigeuner, greife in die Saiten ein!
2. Hochgetürmte Rimaflut, wie bist du so trüb'
3. Wißt ihr, wann mein Kindchen
4. Lieber Gott, du weißt wie oft bereut ich hab'
5. Brauner Bursche führt zum Tanze
6. Röslein dreie in der Reihe blüh'n so rot
7. Kommt dir manchmal in den Sinn
8. Horch, der Wind klagt in den Zweigen traurig sacht
9. Weit und breit schaut Niemand mich an
10. Mond verhüllt sein Angesicht
11. Rote Abendwolken zieh'n

Op. 112/3: Himmel strahlt so helle und klar (trans.)
Op. 112/4: Rote Rosenknospen (trans.)
Op. 112/5: Brennessel steht am Weges Rand (trans.)
Op. 112/6: Liebe Schwalbe, kleine Schwalbe (trans.)

DAUMER, GEORG FRIEDRICH (b. Nuremberg, 1800; d. Würzburg, 1875). Schoolmaster and homeopathic doctor who gave up his post to devote himself to writing. He was an expert on the history of religions and a gifted translator. Principal works were *Frauenbilder und Huldigungen* (1853) and the two collections of translations, *Hafis* (1846) and *Polydora* (1855). Brahms set more works of his than of any other poet.

Op. 52: *Liebeslieder* (trans.)
1. Rede, Mädchen, allzu liebes
2. Am Gesteine rauscht die Flut
3. O die Frauen, o die Frauen
4. Wie des Abends schöne Röte
5. Die grüne Hopfenranke
6. Ein kleiner, hübscher Vogel nahm den Flug
7. Wohl schön bewandt
8. Wenn so lind dein Auge mir
9. Am Donaustrande, da steht ein Haus
10. O, wie sanft die Quelle sich
11. Nein, es ist nicht auszukommen
12. Schlosser auf! und mache Schlösser
13. Vögelein durchrauscht die Luft
14. Sieh, wie ist die Welle klar
15. Nachtigall, sie singt so schön
16. Ein dunkeler Schacht ist Liebe
17. Nicht wandle, mein Licht, dort außen
18. Es bebet das Gesträuche

Op. 64/3: "Fragen" (trans.)
Op. 65: *Neue Liebeslieder* (trans.)
1. Verzicht', o Herz, auf Rettung

2. Finstere Schatten der Nacht
3. An jeder Hand die Finger
4. Ihr schwarzen Augen
5. Wahre, wahre deinen Sohn
6. Rosen steckt mir an die Mutter
7. Vom Gebirge, Well' auf Well'
8. Weiche Gräser im Revier
9. Nagen am Herzen
10. Ich kose süß mit der und der
11. Alles, alles in den Wind
12. Schwarzer Wald, dein Schatten ist so düster!
13. Nein, Geliebter, setze dich
14. Flammenauge, dunkles Haar
Op. 92/1: "O schöne Nacht!" (trans.)

EICHENDORFF, JOSEPH, FREIHERR VON (b. Lubowitz [Upper Silesia], 1788; d. Neiße, 1857). Poet and novelist who ranks among the greatest German Romantic lyricists. The two fundamental influences on his work were a close association with the natural landscape of his youth and his ever-strengthening Roman Catholic faith. His poetry, particularly those works expressing his sensitivity to nature, achieved the popularity of folk song, and his *Aus dem Leben eines Taugenichts* (1826), which combines the dreamlike with the realistic, is a high point of Romantic fiction.
Op. 28/1: "Die Nonne und der Ritter"

GOETHE, JOHANN WOLFGANG VON (b. Frankfurt am Main, 1749; d. Weimar, 1832). The greatest intellectual figure of the German Romantic movement, retaining a lifelong passion for science, philosophy, and politics as well as literature. The sheer number of his writings is remarkable, running to 133 volumes in the Weimar edition. His formative years coincided with the *Sturm und Drang* movement; his later aesthetic theories were sharpened through his association with Schiller.
Op. 28/3: "Es rauschet das Wasser"
Op. 31/1: "Wechsellied zum Tanze"
Op. 61/3: "Phänomen"
Op. 65/15: "Zum Schluß"
Op. 92/4: "Warum?"

GROTH, KLAUS (b. Heide [Dithmarschen], 1819; d. Kiel, 1899). Regional poet and authority on Low German dialect, in which his most famous work, *Quickborn* (1853), is written. His poems have the simplicity of folk songs. He taught literature at Kiel University. Brahms and Groth met in Düsseldorf in 1856 and remained close friends.
Op. 66/1: "Klänge I"
Op. 66/2: "Klänge II"

ḤĀFIZ, MOḤAMMAD SHAMS OD-DĪN (b. Shiraz, c. 1325; d. Shiraz, c. 1390). The most famous lyric poet of Persia. His poetry uses simple though musical language, homely images, and proverbial expressions, and it is characterized by love of humanity and the ability to universalize everyday experience.

Op. 65/2: "Finstere Schatten der Nacht"

HEBBEL, (CHRISTIAN) FRIEDRICH (b. Wesselburen [Dithmarschen], 1813; d. Vienna, 1863). Poet and dramatist, he contributed a new psychological dimension to German drama. He was preoccupied with human existence in isolation, with ethical and metaphysical philosophy, mythology, and religion.

Op. 92/3: "Abendlied"

HERDER, JOHANN GOTTFRIED VON (b. Mohrungen [East Prussia], 1744; d. Weimar, 1803). Critic, theologian, and philosopher, a leading figure in the *Sturm und Drang* movement. He considered poetry to be a natural reaction to the feelings aroused by events; his influence made him a harbinger of the Romantic movement. His *Volkslieder* (1877–1879), retitled *Stimmen der Völker in Liedern* in 1807, was among the important early collections of folk song texts.

Op. 20/1: "Weg der Liebe, I. Teil" (trans.)
Op. 20/2: "Weg der Liebe, II. Teil" (trans.)
Op. 75/1: "Edward" (trans.)

HOFFMANN VON FALLERSLEBEN, AUGUST HEINRICH (b. Fallersleben [Brunswick], 1798; d. Corvey [Weser], 1874). Patriotic poet (his "Deutschland, Deutschland über Alles" was adopted as the German national anthem after World War I), literary historian, and a notable collector and publisher of folk songs. His uncomplicated verses have the qualities of genuine folk literature, and those expressing his love of country and of humanity were of great significance to the German student movement. In the field of ancient Germanic literature, Hoffmann ranks among the most important German scholars.

Op. 28/4: "Der Jäger und sein Liebchen"

HÖLTY, HERMANN (b. Uelzen, 1828; d. Rehburg, 1887). A Hamburg theologian and a grandnephew of Ludwig Hölty, who was one of Brahms's favorite poets. His *Bilder und Balladen* appeared in 1872.

Op. 66/3: "Am Strande"

KELLER, GOTTFRIED (b. Zurich, 1819; d. Zurich, 1890). The greatest German-Swiss writer of the Realist school and a notable lyric poet. He lived for a time as an independent writer in Zurich and was clerk to the canton 1861–1876. Despite his extensive duties as a civil servant, he continued to produce influential poetry, novels, and short stories; his collected works appeared in ten volumes in 1889. Brahms first met him in Switzerland in 1866, and they remained mutually admiring friends—Keller was among the poets with whom Brahms tentatively discussed collaboration on an opera.

WoO posth. 16: *Kleine Hochzeitskantate*

KERNER, JUSTINUS (b. Ludwigsburg, 1786; d. Weinsberg, 1862). Poet, spiritualist, and writer on medicine. He studied medicine in Tübingen and was a friend of Ludwig Uhland, with whom he formed the Swabian group of Romantic poets. His poetry is predominantly somber and shows the influence of folk song.

Op. 61/2: "Klosterfräulein"

KUGLER, FRANZ THEODOR (b. Stettin, 1808; d. Berlin, 1858). Poet, dramatist, biographer of Frederick the Great, and art historian. He studied both literature and architecture, and in 1835 he became a professor at the Akademie der Künste in Berlin. Brahms was a family friend.

Op. 112/1: "Sehnsucht"

Op. 112/2: "Nächtens"

MÖRIKE, EDUARD FRIEDRICH (b. Ludwigsburg, 1804; d. Stuttgart, 1875). One of Germany's greatest lyric poets. He studied theology at Tübingen and held several curacies. His poetry is graceful, original, and often humorous; it reveals superb craftmanship, a virtuoso sense of rhythm, and a rarely equaled subtlety of perception and sincerity of feeling. Among his novels, *Maler Nolten* (1832), itself including several poems, enjoyed great popularity.

Op. 61/1: "Die Schwestern"

MÜLLER, WILHELM (b. Dessau, 1794; d. Dessau, 1827). Scholar, linguist, and a fluent and sensitive lyric poet, now mainly known for the cycles *Die schöne Müllerin* and *Die Winterreise,* set to music by Schubert.

Op. 20/3: "Die Meere" (trans.)

SCHILLER, (JOHANN CHRISTOPH) FRIEDRICH VON (b. Marbach, 1759; d. Weimar, 1805). One of the great German dramatists, poets, and literary theorists. After an early *Sturm und Drang* period, he concentrated increasingly on large-scale historical problems. He was himself a practicing historian, holding a chair at the University of Jena. After 1794 he became a close friend and associate of Goethe.

Op. 64/2: "Der Abend"

SCHMIDT, HANS (b. Fellin [Livonia], 1856; d. Riga, ?). Poet-musician employed as a tutor in Joseph Joachim's house in Berlin. He moved to Vienna in 1881 and studied musical composition with Gustav Nottebohm. Later he worked for several years in Riga as composer, pianist, pedagogue, and critic.

Op. 84/1: "Sommerabend"

Op. 84/2: "Der Kranz"

Op. 84/3: "In den Beeren"

STERNAU, C. O. (pseudonym of Otto Inkermann). No biographical data have survived. His *Gedichte* was published in Berlin in 1851.

Op. 64/1: "An die Heimat"

WENZIG, JOSEPH (b. Prague, 1807; d. Turnau [Bohemia], 1876). Czech patriot and one of the founders of the Bohemian national movement.

His most important work was *Slowakische Volkslieder* (1830); Brahms owned a later edition called *Westslawischer Märchenschatz* (1857).

Op. 31/2: "Neckereien" (trans.)

Op. 31/3: "Der Gang zum Liebchen" (trans.)

Op. 61/4: "Die Boten der Liebe" (trans.)

Op. 75/3: "So laß uns wandern!" (trans.)

ZUCCALMAGLIO, ANTON WILHELM FLORENTIN VON (b. Waldbroel, 1803; d. Nachrodt, 1869). Poet, translator, and folklorist. The son of a lawyer of Italian descent, he also studied law, but he made his living teaching, first in Russia, later in Germany. His principal work (with ANDREAS KRETZSCHMER [1775–1839]), the collection *Deutsche Volkslieder mit ihren Original-Weisen* (1838–1840), was much favored by Brahms, although it subsequently became evident that Zuccalmaglio's tampering had made highly suspect the authenticity of much of its contents.

Op. 84/4: "Vergebliches Ständchen" (adapt.)

Op. 84/5: "Spannung" (adapt.)

FRIENDS AND ASSOCIATES

ALLGEYER, JULIUS (b. Haslach [Kinzigtal], 31 March 1829; d. Munich, 6 September 1900). Engraver and photographer. He first met Brahms in Düsseldorf in 1853 and remained his close friend. He was an ardent champion of both the music of Brahms and the paintings of their mutual friend ANSELM FEUERBACH (1829–1880).

BILLROTH, (CHRISTIAN ALBERT) THEODOR (b. Bergen auf Rügen, 26 April 1829; d. Abbazia [Yugoslavia], 6 February 1894). Professor of surgery in Zurich, where Brahms met him, 1860–1867; thereafter a member of the faculty of the University of Vienna. He was a broadly cultured man and a proficient amateur musician. Many of Brahms's chamber works had their first hearings at the famous soirées in his Vienna home.

BRÜLL, IGNAZ (b. Proßnitz [Moravia], 7 November 1846; d. Vienna, 17 September 1907). Concert pianist and composer. His opera *Das Goldene Kreuz* (1875) had sufficient success to be included in the 1886 repertory of the Metropolitan Opera. He was among Brahms's closest friends, and together they often gave private preliminary two-piano performances of Brahms's orchestral works.

DESSOFF, (FELIX) OTTO (b. Leipzig, 14 January 1835; d. Frankfurt am Main, 28 October 1891). Conductor who led the first performance of Brahms's Symphony No. 1 (Karlsruhe, 4 November 1876). He had been conductor of the Vienna Hofoper and conducted in Karlsruhe from 1875 until his appointment in 1881 as principal conductor at the opera in Frankfurt am Main.

DUSTMANN, (MARIE) LUISE, née MEYER (b. Aix, 1831; d. Berlin, 1899). Operatic soprano. She helped to persuade Brahms to move to Vienna. She made her debut in Breslau in 1849, later appearing regularly at the Vienna Hofoper and in London, Stockholm, Dresden, and Prague; for many years she taught at the Vienna Conservatory.

EBNER-HAUER, OTTILIE. See HAUER, OTTILIE.

FRIEDLÄNDER, MAX (b. Brieg [now Brzeg, Poland], 12 October 1852; d. Berlin, 2 May 1934). Baritone and musicologist. He devoted his life to the study and interpretation of German folk songs and Lieder, and his research yielded many previously unknown Schubert Lieder. He edited the Brahms songs for C. F. Peters and wrote an important book on the Lieder and duets.

GRIMM, JULIUS OTTO (b. Pernau, 6 March 1827; d. Münster, 7 December 1903). Pianist and composer. He studied at the Leipzig Conservatory and was active as a choral conductor in Göttingen (from 1850) and in Münster (from 1860). He and Brahms met in Göttingen in 1853, and together they became closely associated with both Joachim in Hanover and the Schumann circle in Düsseldorf.

HANSLICK, EDUARD (b. Prague, 11 September 1825; d. Baden, 6 August 1904). Critic and writer on music. In 1856 he was appointed lecturer in aesthetics and music history at the University of Vienna, where he became a professor in 1861. He was music critic for the *Wiener Zeitung* 1848–1849, for the *Presse* 1855–1864, and thereafter for the *Neue freie Presse,* retiring from public life in 1895. He embraced the theory of "pure" music, maintaining that the beauty of music is self-contained and not dependent on external factors. He opposed the music drama of Wagner but was a strong champion of Brahms.

HAUER, OTTILIE (b. 3 December 1836; d. 8 July 1920). Soprano whom Brahms met in 1862, shortly after his first arrival in Vienna. Many of his songs were allegedly written for her voice; she was the recipient of at least sixteen Brahms manuscripts. His romantic attachment to her was thwarted when she became engaged to Dr. Edward Ebner on Christmas Day 1863, but the two remained friends.

HERZOGENBERG, (LEOPOLD) HEINRICH (PICOT DE PECCADUC), FREIHERR VON (b. Graz, 10 June 1843; d. Wiesbaden, 9 October 1900). Austrian-born pianist and composer. He taught for a time in Graz but moved in 1872 to Leipzig, where he was one of the founders, later director, of the Bach-Verein; in 1885 he was appointed professor of composition at the Berlin Hochschule. In 1868 he married ELISABETH VON STOCK-HAUSEN (b. Paris, 13 April 1847; d. San Remo, 7 January 1892), a gifted amateur singer and pianist. As a girl she had studied the piano for a short time with Brahms in Vienna, and after her marriage she and her husband resumed the friendship in Leipzig. She became one of Brahms's closest and most trusted friends, one whose musical judgment he often sought.

JOACHIM, JOSEPH (b. Kittsee [Pressburg], 28 June 1831; d. Berlin, 15 August 1907). Famed Hungarian violinist, composer, and conductor. A close friend and champion of Brahms, he lived successively in Leipzig, Weimar, Hanover, and Berlin. In 1863 he married the concert and operatic contralto AMALIE SCHNEEWEISS (b. Marburg, 10 May 1839; d. Berlin, 3 February 1899), who made her debut in Troppau in 1853. Under the stage name Weiss she sang from 1854 at the Kärntnerthor Theater in Vienna and from 1862 at the Royal Opera in Hanover. From 1866 she devoted herself exclusively to the concert hall and became known as an eminent Lieder singer.

KALBECK, MAX (b. Breslau, 4 January 1850; d. Vienna, 5 May 1921). Writer and music critic. Between 1870 and 1890 he published several volumes of poetry; after 1875 he was critic for various German and Austrian newspapers. He first met Brahms in Breslau in 1874, later becoming one of his most frequent companions in Vienna. He was the author of the standard biography of Brahms and edited several volumes of his correspondence.

LEVI, HERMANN (b. Giessen, 7 November 1839; d. Munich, 13 May 1900). Conductor and composer. After conducting posts in Saarbrücken, Mannheim, Rotterdam, and Karlsruhe (where he befriended both Clara Schumann and Brahms), he was from 1872 to 1896 conductor of the Court Theater in Munich. He was a renowned interpreter of Brahms and was also among the greatest of the early Bayreuth conductors.

MANDYCZEWSKI, EUSEBIUS (b. Czernowitz [now Chernovtsy], 18 August 1857; d. Vienna, 13 July 1929). Musicologist. He became conductor of the Vienna Singakademie, archivist of the Gesellschaft der Musikfreunde, and professor of music at the Vienna Conservatory. He met Brahms in 1879 while a student in Vienna and became his close friend and secretarial assistant. He was joint editor (with HANS GÁL [1890–1987]) of the Gesamtausgabe of Brahms's works (1926–1928).

OPHÜLS, GUSTAV (1866–1926). Jurist and one of the circle of Brahms's friends in Krefeld. At Brahms's suggestion he made a compilation of the texts of the vocal works, the manuscript of which, with drawings by WILLY VON BECKERATH (1868–1938), he gave as a gift to the composer in December 1896. The *Brahms-Texte* were published, after Brahms's death, in Leipzig in 1898; an expanded and corrected edition was printed in Berlin in 1908 and 1923, and a modern edition was published in Ebenhausen bei München in 1983.

RUDORFF, ERNST FRIEDRICH KARL (b. Berlin, 18 January 1840; d. Berlin, 31 December 1916). Pianist and composer. His teachers included Clara Schumann and Ignaz Moscheles. He headed the piano division of the Berlin Hochschule from 1869 to 1910 and directed the Sternschen Gesangverein from 1880 to 1890. At his request Brahms arranged a suite of *Liebeslieder* for small orchestra and SATB soli or chorus.

SCHUBRING, ADOLF (1817–1893). Judge by profession, music critic by avocation. His series of articles in the *Neue Zeitschrift für Musik,* spread over five issues in the spring of 1862, constituted the first thorough assessment of the young Brahms's work.

SCHUMANN, CLARA JOSEPHINE, née WIECK (b. Leipzig, 13 September 1819; d. Frankfurt am Main, 20 May 1896). The foremost woman pianist of her time and a gifted composer. She was the daughter and pupil of FRIEDRICH WIECK (1785–1873), the wife of ROBERT SCHUMANN (1810–1856), and the lifelong friend and confidante of Brahms. After her husband's death she lived in Berlin and in Baden-Baden and, with Brahms, edited the Schumann Gesamtausgabe for Breitkopf & Härtel.

SIEBOLD, AGATHE VON (1833–1909). Daughter of a Göttingen professor, she met Brahms in 1858 through Julius and Philippine Grimm. Brahms was greatly attracted to her but could not bring himself to marry her, and they parted painfully in January 1859. Late in life she novelized the unfortunate affair under the title *Erinnerungen.*

SIMROCK, FRIEDRICH AUGUST [FRITZ] (b. Bonn, 2 January 1837; d. Ouchy, 20 August 1901). Junior partner in N. Simrock, the Bonn music publishing firm founded by his grandfather, Nicolaus, which after 1860 published most of Brahms's music. He became head of the business in 1870 and relocated it to Berlin. Brahms regarded him as a good friend and entrusted him with the management of his finances.

SPENGEL, JULIUS HEINRICH (b. Hamburg, 12 June 1853; d. Hamburg, 17 April 1936). Choir director, teacher, and composer. He taught in Hamburg and from 1878 to 1927 conducted the Hamburg Cäcilienverein, which gave the first performance of the four *Zigeunerlieder* of Op. 112 in 1892.

STOCKHAUSEN, ELISABETH VON. See HERZOGENBERG, (LEOPOLD) HEINRICH.

STOCKHAUSEN, JULIUS (CHRISTIAN) (b. Paris, 22 July 1826; d. Frankfurt am Main, 22 September 1906). Baritone singer of French opera and German Lieder, conductor, and teacher. After he met Brahms in 1856 they often concertized together. Many of Brahms's Lieder, including the *Magelone* romances, Op. 33, were written for him, and he was the baritone soloist in the first performance of *Ein deutsches Requiem* in 1868. In 1863 Stockhausen was chosen over Brahms to be conductor of the Hamburg Philharmonic concerts.

WALTER, GUSTAV (b. Bilin [Bohemia], 11 February 1834; d. Vienna, 30 January 1910). A lyric tenor, he sang at the Vienna Hofoper from 1856 to 1887. He was also an esteemed Lieder singer, and he took part in first performances of many of Brahms's songs as well as of the cantata *Rinaldo,* Op. 50, in 1869.

WILT, MARIE, née LIEBENTHALER (b. Vienna, 30 January 1833; d. Vienna, 24 September 1891). Dramatic soprano and a member of the Vienna Singverein from 1859 to 1865. She took part in Brahms's first concert in Vienna (6 January 1863) and became one of his favorite interpreters of his music.

ZUR MÜHLEN, RAIMUND VON (b. Livonia, 10 November 1854; d. Steyning [Sussex], 9 December 1931). Tenor and pedagogue. He attended the Berlin Hochschule für Musik, studied with Stockhausen in Frankfurt am Main, and coached Lieder interpretation with Clara Schumann. From 1905 until his death he lived in England, where he had his greatest success.

SELECTED BIBLIOGRAPHY

Atlas, Raphael. "Text and Musical Gesture in Brahms's Vocal Duets and Quartets with Piano." *Journal of Musicology* 10, no. 2 (spring 1992): 231–60.

Barkan, Hans, trans. and ed. *Johannes Brahms and Theodor Billroth: Letters from a Musical Friendship.* Norman: University of Oklahoma Press, 1957.

Bell, A. Craig. *Brahms: The Vocal Music.* Madison, NJ: Fairleigh Dickinson University Press, 1996.

Boyd, Jack Arthur. "Secular Music for the Solo Vocal Ensemble in the Nineteenth Century." Ph.D. diss., University of Iowa, 1971.

Bozarth, George. "Brahms's Duets for Soprano and Alto, Op. 61." *Studia Musicologica* 25 (1983): 191–210.

Brodbeck, David. "Brahms as Editor and Composer: His Two Editions of Ländler by Schubert and His First Two Cycles of Waltzes, Opera 39 and 52." Ph.D. diss., University of Pennsylvania, 1984.

———. "Compatibility, Coherence, and Closure in Brahms's *Liebeslieder* Waltzes." *Explorations in Music, the Arts, and Ideas: Essays in Honor of Leonard B. Meyer,* ed. Eugene Narmour and Ruth A. Solie, 411–37. Stuyvesant, NY: Pendragon Press, 1988.

Evans, Edwin. *Handbook to the Vocal Works of Johannes Brahms.* New York: Lenox Hill (Burt Franklin), 1970. Reprint of the 1912 edition.

Friedländer [Friedlaender], Max. *Brahms's Lieder.* Trans. C. Leonard Leese. New York: AMS Press, 1976. Reprint of the 1928 London edition.

Fuller-Maitland, J. A. *Brahms.* London: Methuen, 1911.

Gál, Hans. *Johannes Brahms: Werke und Persönlichkeit.* Frankfurt am Main: Fischer Bücherei, 1961. Trans. Joseph Stein as *Johannes Brahms: His Work and Personality.* New York: Alfred A. Knopf, 1971.

Geiringer, Karl. *Brahms: His Life and Work.* 3rd ed. New York: Da Capo Press, 1982.

Johannes Brahms Briefwechsel. 16 vols. Rev. eds. Berlin: Deutsche Brahms-Gesellschaft, 1906–1922. Reprint, Tutzing: Hans Schneider, 1974.

Kalbeck, Max. *Johannes Brahms.* 4 vols. Rev. eds. Berlin: Deutsche Brahms-Gesellschaft, 1912–1921. Reprint, Tutzing: Hans Schneider, 1976.

———, ed. *Johannes Brahms: The Herzogenberg Correspondence.* Trans. Hannah Bryant. New York: Vienna House, 1971. Reprint of the 1909 London edition.

Keys, Ivor. *Johannes Brahms.* Portland: Amadeus Press, 1989.

Litzmann, Berthold, ed. *Letters of Clara Schumann and Johannes Brahms, 1853–1896.* 2 vols. New York: Vienna House, 1973. Reprint of the 1927 New York edition.

MacDonald, Malcolm. *Brahms.* New York: Schirmer Books, 1990.

May, Florence. *The Life of Johannes Brahms.* 2 vols. 2nd ed., rev. London: William Reeves, 1948. Reprint, Neptune City, NJ: Paganiniana, 1981.

McCorkle, Margit L., and Donald M. McCorkle. *Johannes Brahms: thematisch-bibliographisches Werkverzeichnis.* Munich: G. Henle Verlag, 1984.

Musgrave, Michael, ed. *Brahms 2: Biographical, Documentary and Analytical Studies.* Cambridge: Cambridge University Press, 1987.

———. *The Music of Brahms.* London: Routledge & Kegan Paul, 1985.

Niemann, Walter. *Brahms*. Berlin: Schuster & Loeffler, 1920. Trans. Catherine Alison Phillips. New York: Alfred A. Knopf, 1929. Reprint, New York: Cooper Square Publishers, 1969.

Ophüls, Gustav. *Brahms-Texte: vollständige Sammlung der von Johannes Brahms componirten und musikalisch bearbeiteten Dichtungen.* 2nd ed. Berlin: Verlag der Deutschen Brahms-Gesellschaft, 1908.

Stark, Lucien. *A Guide to the Solo Songs of Johannes Brahms.* Bloomington: Indiana University Press, 1995.

INDEX OF TITLES AND FIRST LINES

(Titles of cycles and entire works are in italics. Songs with titles are indexed by title [in quotation marks] and by first line. Songs without titles are indexed by first line.)

INDEX OF NAMES

LUCIEN STARK, Professor Emeritus of Piano at the University of Kentucky, maintains a full schedule of coaching and performing. He is the author of *A Guide to the Solo Songs of Johannes Brahms*.